WOMEN
IN INDIAN MYTHOLOGY

Also by the same author

The Eminent Indian Series:
Administrators and Political Thinkers
Freedom Fighters
Litterateurs
Scientists and Technologists
Revolutionaries
Musicians
Film Personalities

Gurus: Ancient, Medieval and Modern

WOMEN
IN INDIAN MYTHOLOGY

M.L. Ahuja

Rupa & Co

Copyright © M.L. Ahuja 2011

Published 2011 by
Rupa Publications India Pvt. Ltd.
7/16, Ansari Road, Daryaganj
New Delhi 110 002

Sales Centres:

Allahabad Bengaluru Chennai
Hyderabad Jaipur Kathmandu
Kolkata Mumbai

Typeset by
Televijay Technologies Pvt. Ltd.
New No. 30, Chamiers Road,
Nandanam,
Chennai 600 035

Printed in India by
Saurabh Printers Pvt. Ltd.
A-16, Sector-IV,
Noida 201 301

Contents

Preface

Right from the days of Vedas, women have not lagged behind men. During the Vedic period, many of them were epitomes of intellectual and spiritual attainment. They complemented and supplemented their male partners. Vedic wisdom is encapsulated in myriad hymns—twenty-seven women-seers emerged from them. Some of them have been the basis for inspiration to both men and women for centuries.

Of all the organised religions of the world, women have perhaps the most prominent presence in Hinduism, both visible as well as invisible. As sages, women have borne the revealed word. As spiritual and religious teachers, Hindu women have sustained our dharma in various ways down the ages. As noble queens and as warriors, Hindu women have protected our faith from disintegrating into extinction. As musicians, dancers, and artists, they have been the embodiment of all that is beautiful. As mothers, they have been our first teachers. As wives, they have provided the locus around which family and social life revolves. As daughters, they have taught us compassion and as our guides, they have made many men into great human beings.

While it is true that in Vedas, the word *man* is used in a generic manner to denote 'human beings', authoritative grammar and ritual texts emphasise that this is merely a figure of speech, and that man and woman together constitute two halves of the same person while performing Vedic sacred rites between man and woman. The language in which the revealed Hindu texts are composed, namely, Sanskrit, has a neuter gender in addition to the masculine and feminine. In fact, the ultimate reality, the Supreme God of Hindus, is often described as neutral gender. A verse of *Rigveda* says that all the various deities are but descriptions of One Truth (*ekam sat*), and it is in neuter gender as if to emphasise that God is not male. *Gayatri Mantra*, the holiest prayer of Hindus, in classical Hinduism in Vedas, is often represented symbolically as a *devi*. She is thus a female deity, who is also often termed as the Mother of all Vedas, and giver of boons.

In scriptures, God is described like the husband of all human beings. In Vedas, however, we even read that God is like a dear wife whom the worshipper loves like a doting husband. The divine word itself is likened to a beautiful maiden who manifests her beauty to the husband.

As goddesses (*devis*), women are worshipped as mothers of even the most powerful male deities (*devtas*). Devi Aditi is thus the mother of all prominent *devatas*, such as Varuna, Mitra, Aryaman, Rudras, Indra, of kings, and many other excellent sons. She is invoked as the mistress of the Cosmic Order, omnipotent, protector, mother of the devout worshipper, and a wise guide of all humans. In Vedas, *devatas* are hardly mentioned without corresponding *devis*. Almost, as a rule, the sage, the worshipper, and the ritualist invoke *devatas* to manifest along with *devis*, and partake in the sacred oblations poured into the sacred fire altar.

The *Ramayana* illustrates the inseparability of Lord Narayana and Lakshmi. It shows that when we surrender to God, it must be to the *divya dampati* (divine couple), and it is not possible to think of the Lord without His consort or vice versa. When King Janaka offers Sita's hand in marriage to Rama, he says, *Iyam Sita Mame Sutaa Sahadharma Chaaree Tava.* Here he says that Sita will help Rama carry out his dharma. When Rama prepares to leave for the forest, Lakshmana addresses both Rama and Sita, saying that while he (Rama) spends time in the company of Vaidehi, he (Lakshmana) will serve them in their waking hours, and when they are asleep. Thus, Lakshmana shows that one must adopt equal attitude to the Lord and the Goddess Mahalakshmi. The observance of Akampana and Soorpanaka in the epic also shows the inseparability of Rama and Sita. Akampana says if Ravana wants to defeat Rama, he must take Sita away from him. Soorpanaka goes a step further. Though she is a demoness she reveals through her words her grasp of the concept of godhead. Though Ravana, a learned person, might have conquered many worlds, there may be many who pay him obeisance, but he lacks the most essential requisite of the *Parabrahmam*, the presence of Lakshmi. Again, when Anjaneya goes to Lanka (now, Sri Lanka), and sees Sita, he conjures up a mental image of Rama and Sita as a couple and remarks that they match each other in all respects. Anjaneya says that Rama and Sita are able to bear the pangs of separation only because Sita remains enthroned in Rama's heart and he in hers. When he returns to Rama after meeting Sita, Anjaneya first turns in the direction of Lanka and worships Sita, before he turns towards Rama and prostrates before him.

Again, the Divine Mother is termed as *Shakti* or the 'Supreme Power', as 'Uma' or the sacred wisdom, as Maheshvari or the supreme goddess, etc. In numerous iconic representations, God is shown as *ardhanarishvara* or 'God who is half woman', to emphasise that either God has no gender or he is both man and woman. Even male deities, such as Lord Vishnu, sometimes incarnate as a women to serve the cause of dharma. The *devi* herself is often said to combine the powers of all male deities including Brahma, Vishnu, and Shiva.

In the Vaishnava tradition, which is the most prevalent Hindu tradition today, God, as explained above, is worshipped as Vishnu together with 'Shri', who is also addressed variously as 'Lakshmi'. They incarnate together and their incarnations, namely, that of Rama and Sita, respectively, and so on, are also worshipped as a couple. Their equal reverence can be assessed from the words of sage Parashar, 'O Maitreyi! Always a companion of Vishnu and the Mother of this Universe, Devi Lakshmi is eternal. Vishnu is omnipresent, so is She. If she is speech, Vishnu is the object of description. Vishnu is the law, and she is the policy. Lord Vishnu is knowledge, she is intelligence; he is dharma, she is good *karma*; if Vishnu is the creator, she is the creation that abides eternally with him. He is the mountain, she is earth. He is the virtue of contentment, she is the all-satisfying. If Lord Vishnu is desire, she is the object of desire. He is the sacred Vedic ritual, she is the priestly fee … '

Lord Rama is worshipped with his wife Sita. Lord Krishna is worshipped with Radha or with Devi Rukmini. Again, when God is worshipped as a divine couple by Hindus, the name of the feminine typically precedes that of masculine. For instance, we worship 'Sita–Ram', 'Radhe–Shyam', 'Uma–Mahesh' or 'Shri–Vishnu', and so on. In the sacred stories of Hindu texts, Ganesha is considered more as his mother Parvati's son than that of his father, Shiva. According to some versions, Parvati created Ganesh out of her own power because she wanted a son whom only she could call her own. Ganesh is typically worshipped as a child, and is often depicted along with his brother, Skanda, together with their all-powerful mother.

In numerous Hindu communities of Bangladesh, Nepal, and India, Durga Puja, the most prominent festival in the year is dedicated to the Divine Mother. During Diwali, the most important festival in northern India and amongst Hindu communities in the Caribbean, the man worship is offered to Devi Lakshmi. Diwali itself is often called 'Lakshmi Puja'. A period of nine nights every year is devoted to the worship of numerous manifestations of the Mother. It is celebrated as Durga Puja festival in eastern India and as Navaratri in Gujarat as the major festival.

For Hindus, God is not essentially a fatherly figure. He is mother and father combined. In Hindu mythology, nature and earth are uniformly referred to as Mother Nature (*Prakriti*) and kindly mother earth (*Prithvi Mata*). God and nature are sometimes depicted as husband and wife who create the inanimate and animate universe together just as mother and father give birth to children. The words of sage Parashar in a hymn should make it further clear, 'O Earth, my Mother, establish me securely in spiritual and material happiness, and in full account with Heaven. O Wise One! Uphold me in grace and splendour.'

It has been held traditionally that Devi Annapurna is the presiding deity of food grains. It is in sharp contrast to the prevalent view in most of the cases that man is bread-earner in the family. Similarly, forests that provide us many resources are said to be presided over by *devis* who are known as *Vanadevis* (vana = forest). There are numerous Hindu rituals involving the veneration of trees, plants, and forests in their feminine form.

It is Mother Ganga, Mother Yamuna, Mother Kaveri, and so on, who have manifested as rivers to feed mankind. Rivers, their confluences, and their origins form prominent Hindu pilgrim centres. The evening worship of Mother Ganges in the pilgrim centre of Haridwar with hundreds of lamps set afloat on the river at night is a mesmerising spectacle.

India is termed as motherland and not fatherland. It is in recognition of the fact that the land we live in sustains us in the same way as our own mother. We, in India, worship our country as *Bharatmata*. According to a verse attributed to Lord Rama, one's mother as well as motherland are more exalted than Heaven. When a family enters their new home, they invoke God with a request to dwell therein in a benevolent feminine form to make it come alive. Household women play a leading role in this ceremony, and the wife is the first one to enter the new home, as the wife is regarded as *grihyalakshmi* or the embodiment of Devi Lakshmi.

The close connection of women with Vedas, the text regarded as divine revelation in Hindu dharma, may be judged from the fact that out of the 407 sages associated with the revelation of *Rigveda*, twenty-one are women. Many of these *mantras* (hymns) are quite significant. An invocatory *mantra* of the *Atharvaveda* addresses divinity as a *devi*, the Goddess who, while present in waters, fulfills all our desires and hopes. In the *Atharvaveda*, the entire fourteenth book dealing with marriages, domestic issues, etc. is attributed to a woman sage. Portions of other nineteen books are also attributed to women sages.

Both male and female deities are extolled in the hymns of all revealed texts of Hindus and in the family prayers of all the ten lineages of Vedic sages. Numerous schools of Vedic tradition customarily offer homage to women sages during their daily prayers. The superlative epithets used uniformly to denote female deities like Ushas, Saraswati, etc., in Vedas describe them as sweetly smiling, the first or foremost of deities to whom worship is offered, the shining ones, splendid and beautiful, possessors of wisdom, teachers of mankind, and as powers capable of fulfilling the desires of human beings.

The foremost of Vedic women seers had been Ghosha, the granddaughter of Dirghatamas and daughter of Kakshivat. Her implorations with Ashwins and the devotion of her forefathers towards them made them cure her disease and allow her to experience wedded bliss. The long conversations of sage Agasthya and his wife Lopamudra narrated in the *Rigveda* testify to the great intelligence of Lopamudra. Maitreyi contributed towards the enhancement of her sage husband Yajnavalkya's personality. Gargi, the Vedic prophetess and daughter of sage Vachaknu, composed several hymns that questioned the origin of all existence.

Madalasa, the daughter of Vishvasu, the Gandharva king, was a great inspiration to her son, Ritdhvaj. When Shatrujit died, Ritdhvaj took the position of king and engaged in the royal duties. She enlightened her son with spiritual knowledge in songs she sang to him. Sati, the daughter of Prajapati Daksha, from the *Puranas*, did not tolerate the dishonour of her husband Lord Shiva. Anusuya was a woman who could bring back the life of a dead sage due to the power of her own austerity and devotion to her husband. She showed that devotion to a qualified husband gives the wife fame, power, and is the fulfillment of her dharma. Sita in the *Ramayana* is the perfect example of womanly and wifely virtues and holds one of the highest places among women in Vedic culture and of women's character. Draupadi in the *Mahabharata* is the epitome of righteousness. The devotion of Savitri to her husband, Satyavan, saved her husband from Yama, the god of death. In the *Kena Upanishad*, knowledge appears as Uma, a woman, to dispel the ignorance of Indra. Parvati, through her intense austerities, was able to match Shiva's awesome powers by creating incredible energy in her yoga meditations and gain enough energy to attract the attention of the supreme deity, Brahma. After marriage with Shiva, Parvati inspired her consort to accept pleasure into his life and become the patron of arts. Shiva now became the Lord of Dance ensuring that the energy created by his asceticism was channelled for the entertainment of all mankind.

No better example of male–female love in this world can be cited than that of Gopi-Krishna love. Gopi-Krishna love has been likened to passionate and self-less love of a devotee towards the Supreme Being. Love is God because the best thing of true happiness we know on earth is love. Ego simply does not exist with love. Love fulfills the heart so deeply that it ceases to yearn for anything else. Our soul desires to grow in love, but if our subconscious mind hides so many ambitions, they impede its growth. An innocent Gopi-like housewife leaves the care of all the major problems to her husband. She relaxes, realising that her Master is a greater power to take care of her. The foremost concern of Gopis is to love Krishna like Gopi-souls with all their heart, soul, and mind. Mahamati Prannath, who brought new dimension to Hinduism during Aurangzeb's time, said that womanhood of a Gopi is an acceptable form of mental framework to reach the supreme lover Krishna of Paramdham. The tradition of Gopi-Krishna worship by saints like Surdas, Meera, and Mahamati Prannath and the description of *Raas-Lila* indirectly reminds us that we do not know of any other phenomenon where we lose ourselves so completely and through which we could describe in human language of what happens to the soul when she loses herself completely into the supreme bliss of love plays of Krishna and Gopis. To this, the Vedantis say that the river has merged into the ocean, and the Buddhists say that the river has just disappeared. Marriage among Hindus, therefore, is analogous to merging of two noble souls where each one has to be oblivious of one's individuality.

In the Hindu tradition, among women from the *Mahabharata* and the *Ramayana*, who are especially revered, are the following: Draupadi, Tara, Ahalya, Mandodari, Sita, Savitri, Sati, and Damayanti. They are worshipped by Hindus as divine women of dharma, noted for unwavering devotion to their husbands, and for standing by them through all ups and downs in their lives. These together with Maitreyi and Gargi, described above, should be an inspiration to the succeeding generations. Keeping this in view, the following pages of this book, *Women in Hindu Mythology*, bring to focus values that some of the feminine characters in Vedas, the *Ramayana*, and the *Mahabhara* cherished with the hope that the succeeding generations shall follow their footsteps.

In my efforts to present before you the lives and contributions of all such women, I have consulted a number of books from various libraries, particularly that of Jamia Milia Islamia University in New Delhi. I am grateful to the University Librarian, Dr Gyas-ud-din Makdooni and his staff members for giving me an access to books in the library. I would like to thank Mr Kapish Mehra, Managing Director of Rupa Publications

India Pvt. Ltd. for undertaking publication of this book. My wife, Mrs Asha Ahuja, also deserves my thanks for cooperating with me in my efforts to concentrate on this project. I also received continued encouragement from H. E. Dr Bhishama Narain Singh, former Cabinet Minister and Governor of Tamil Nadu, Dr GVG Krishnamurty, former Election Commissioner of India, and Mr Saurabh Bhagat, Dr Rahul Malhotra, Mrs Lovelina Bhagat and Dr Chetna Malhotra among my family members. The illustrations in this book have been prepared by Deepak. My thanks are due to all such persons. My thanks are also due to various other people who helped me in one way or the other.

M.L. Ahuja
Delhi
22 February 2011

Ambika

A mbika is a benign form of the goddess, one of the central deities of the Shakta region, along with Durga, Kali, and Parvati. She is a woman of respect and distinction. She was the daughter of King Kashi and wife of Vichitravirya, king of Hastinapur. In the *Mahabharata* epic, Pandu is the son of Vichitravirya from his second wife, Ambika, from Ved Vyasa, the author of the *Mahabharata*.

According to a story in the *Mahabharata*, Queen Satyavati bore King Shantanu two sons, Chitrangada and Vichitravirya. Satyavati was the second wife of Shantanu, the first being Ganga who gave birth to Bhishma. Bhishma was born as the eldest son of the King Shantanu by Ganga. Bhishma means one who has taken a terrible oath. It refers to his vow of life-long celibacy. Originally named Devratha, he became known as Bhishma after he took the *bhishan pratigya* (terrible oath)—the vow of life-long celibacy and of service to whoever sat on the throne of his father (the throne of Hastinapur). He took this oath so that his father, Shantanu could marry a fisherwoman Satyavati—Satyavati's father had refused to give his daughter's hand to Shantanu on the grounds that his daughter's children would never be rulers as Shantanu already had a son, Devratha. This made Shantanu despondent and upon discovering the reason for his father's despondency, Devratha sought out the girl's father and promised him that he would never stake a claim to the throne, implying that the child born to Shantanu and Satyavati would become the ruler after Shantanu. At this, Satyavati's father retorted that even if Devratha gave up his claim to the throne, his (Devratha's) children would still claim the throne. Devratha then took the terrible vow of life-long celibacy, thus sacrificing his 'crown-prince' title and denying himself the pleasures of intercourse. This gave him immediate recognition among the gods and his father granted him the boon of *Swachhanda Mrityu* (control over his own death—he could choose the time of his death, but he was not immortal). Bhishma also took another vow shortly after the marriage of Shantanu and Satyavati. He vowed that he would see his father's image in whoever sat on the throne of Hastinapur and would serve him without question.

When Shantanu died, Vichitravirya and Chitrangada were too young to inherit the throne. Therefore, Bhishma, the eldest son, took up the responsibility and became the interim king. Later, Chitrangada, the eldest son, succeeded Shantanu to the throne of Hastinapur. When he died childless, the second son, Vichitravirya, became king. As Vichitravirya was still a child when he was crowned king, Bhishma ruled as his regent. When the young king attained the proper age to marry, Bhishma searched for a suitable bride for him. And he heard that the king of Kasi was holding a *swayamvara* for his three daughters. Since Vichitravirya himself was yet too young to stand any chance of being chosen by the young women, Bhishma himself went to the *swayamvara*.

Bhishma won the *swayamvara* for Vichitravirya and brought the Princesses Amba, Ambika, and Ambalika to marry the latter. But Amba had already given her heart to the Raja of Salva. Therefore, Bhishma sent her to the Raja. The Raja, however, rejected her because she had been in another man's house. Deeply hurt, Amba retired to the forest to practice extreme austerities in order that she might gain the power to avenge the wrong done to her by Bhishma. She ended her life voluntarily on a funeral pyre and was reborn as Shikhandi, who slew Bhishma eventually in the great battle between the Kauravas and Pandavas.

Therefore, Ambika and Ambalika were married to Vichitravirya. Unfortunately, shortly after his marriage, Vichitravirya died of tuberculosis. As he died without any heir, Satyavati asked Bhishma to produce the next generation by Vichitravirya's wives, Ambika and Ambalika. But Bhishma declined this as he had already vowed to remain celibate during his life.

Satyavati, who needed to ensure that the line of succession was carried on, called upon her other son, Vyasa, to go to the beds of two queens and father children. Vyasa was considered an ideal Brahmarishi—omniscient, truthful, purest of the pure, and possessor of knowledge of the essence of Brahman. Vyasa wanted the queens Ambika and Ambalika to come alone to him. First, did Ambika, but because of her shyness and fear she closed her eyes. Vyasa told Satyavati that the child would be born blind. Later, this child was named Dhritrarashtra. Thus, Satyavati sent Ambalika and warned her that she should remain calm. But Ambalika's face became pale because of fear. Vyasa told that the child would suffer from anaemia and would not be fit to rule the kingdom. Later, this child was named Pandu. Then Vyasa told Satyavati to send one of them again so that a healthy child could be born. This time Ambika and Ambalika sent their maid in the place of themselves. The maid was quite calm and composed during the yogic process, and so she got a healthy child, later named as Vidura, who became a fearless and intelligent *mahamantri* of Dhritrarashtra inheriting greater attributes of his biological father.

Goddess Ambika finds mention as *Vajasaneyi Samhita* where she is addressed as the sister of the God Rudra and is invoked to come and partake of her share in the sacrifice along with Rudra. This invocation is repeated in the *Taitiriya Brahmanya*. In the *Maitrayani Samhita*, Ambika is referred to be the sister as well as the *yoni* (mother) female counterpart of Rudra. In the *Taittirya Brahmana*, and both the *Maitrayani* and the *Kathaka Samhita*, Ambika, as the sister of Rudra, has been identified with the autumn. When Ambika was identified with Durga, the autumnal worship of the goddess became a widespread custom.

In the *Atharva Veda*, in a hymn, Ambika is addressed as the great mother goddess (*Devi*). It became evident that the great goddess is the manifestation of everything that possesses brilliance and power, and that she is the mother even of Indra, i.e., the power underlying the might even of the mightiest of gods. We also find that the goddess was named Uma, one of the most famous names of the great goddess of India. The word 'Uma' denotes the goddess who measures Shiva, i.e., the Shakti of Shiva. Kalidasa says in his *Kumara Sambhava* that Parvati, the goddess, as the daughter of the mountain, was dissuaded by her mother, Menaka, from resorting to austere penance for Shiva for Parvati. Uma also stands for the knowledge of Brahman. The word *Ambika-pataye* (to the lord of Ambika) is found in the *Taittiriya Aranyaka*.

In the form of Parvati, Ambika is known as the divine spouse of Lord Shiva and is the mother of her two sons, Ganesha and Kartikeya, and daughter Jyoti. As destroyer of the powerful demon Mahish and all his great commanders, she is worshipped during an annual festival called Durga Puja, especially popular among Bengalis. It is believed that when demonic forces create imbalance, all gods unite becoming one divine force called Shakti or Durga. Uma or Parvati, other names of Ambika, seem to be the basis of legends in *Puranas* with whom most of the other mother goddesses were associated or have merged themselves. The evolution of the idea and philosophy of *Shakti* greatly helped this process of identification and unification. As the Shakti is fundamentally one, the mother must also be one; the mothers were necessarily intermingled and unified. Uma or Parvati, as the consort or the inseparable counterpart of Lord Shiva, seems to have attained wide prominence by the beginning of the Christian era. Kalidasa began his great epic *Raghuvansham* with a salute to Parvati–Parameshwara, the mother and father of the universe, who are said to be eternally and inseparably related to each other just as a word and its meaning are.

Ambika is the active power of manifest energy of Shiva that pervades the entire existence. Its most refined aspect is Parashakti or Satchidananda, the pure consciousness and primal substratum of all forms. This pristine divine energy unfolds as the power of desire, will, and love, *kriya shakti* (the power of action), *ichha shakti* (the power of will) and *jnana shakti* (the power of wisdom, knowing), represented as the three prongs of Shiva's *trishul* or trident. From these arise the five powers of revealment, concealment, dissolution, preservation, and creation.

In *Saiva Siddhanta*, Shiva is all, and his divine energy, Shakti, is inseparable from him. This unity is symbolised in the image of *Ardhanarishvara*, 'half-female God'. In popular Hinduism, the unity of Shiva and Shakti is replaced with the concept of Shiva and Shakti as separate entities. Shakti is represented as female and Shiva as male. In Hindu temples, art and mythology are seen everywhere as the divine couple. This depiction has its source in the folk-narrative sections of the *Puranas*, where it is given elaborate expression. Shakti is personified in many forms as the consorts of gods. For example, the goddesses Parvati, Lakshmi, and Saraswati are the respective mythological consorts of Shiva, Vishnu, and Brahma.

Within the Shakta religion, the worship of the goddess is paramount, in her fierce and benign forms. Shakti is the divine mother of manifest creation, visualised as a female form, and Shiva is specifically the unmanifest absolute. The fierce or black forms of the goddess include Kali, Durga, Chandi, Chamundi, Bhadrakali, and Bhairavi. The benign or white forms include Uma, Gauri, Ambika, Parvati, Maheshvari, Lalita, and Annapurna. As Rajarajeshvari (divine queen of kings), she is the presiding deity of the Sri Chakra yantra. She is also worshipped as the ten Mahavidyas, manifestations of the highest knowledge—Kali, Tara, Shodashi, Bhuvaneshvah, Chinnamasta, Bhairavi, Dhumavati, Bagata, Matangi, and Kamala. While some Shaktas view these as individual beings, most revere them as manifestations of the singular Devi. There are also numerous minor goddess forms, in the category of *gramadevata* (village deity). They include Pitari, 'snake-catcher' (usually represented by a simple stone) and Mariyamman, 'smallpox goddess'.

After the death of Shiva's first love Sati, Shiva was so distraught that he rejected the world outside and isolated himself into a dark cave, buried amongst the snow-covered peaks of the Himalayas. Meanwhile, the demons, lead by Taraka, rose from the netherworld and drove the *Devas*, gods, out of the heavens. The gods sought a warrior who would help them regain the celestial realm. Brahma felt convinced that only Shiva could father such a warrior. But Shiva was immersed in meditation. As he performed *tapas* (austerities), meditations, that produce great heat and energy, his mind was filled with great knowledge and his body became resplendent with energy. But all this was of no use. The gods, therefore, invoked the mother goddess, who appeared before them as *Kundalini*, a coiled serpent. The serpent coiled herself around Shiva, weaned out his knowledge, and energy for the good of the world and made him father a child. Shakti took birth as Parvati, daughter of the Himavan, lord of the mountains, determined to draw Shiva out of his cave and make him her consort. Parvati went into the forest and performed rigorous *tapas*, wearing nothing to protect her tender body, eating nothing, not even a leaf, thus earning the admiration of forest ascetics who named her Aparna. Aparna matched Shiva in her capacity to cut herself from the world.

The power of her *tapas* shook Shiva out of his meditation. He
stepped out of his cave and accepted Parvati as his wife. Kama
and then six-headed Kartikeya were born out of their wedlock.
Parvati taught Kartikeya the art of war and turned him into
the celestial warlord called Skanda. Skanda took command of
the celestial armies, defeated Taraka in battle, and restored the
heavens to the gods.

Goddess Ambika is also called Durga, which is yet
another form of Shakti. Durga in Sanskrit means one who is
incomprehensible or difficult to reach. She is worshipped for
her gracious as well as terrifying aspect. Mother of the universe,
she represents the infinite power of the universe and is a symbol
of a female dynamism. The manifestation of Durga is said to
emerge from her formless essence and the two are inseparable.

According to a legend associated with Chamunda Devi
Temple, two demons, Chanda and Munda of Shumbh Nishumbh,
the notorious demon kings, with their wicked mind, tried to
harass the goddess Ambika. A battle ensued between the gods
and demons. Chamunda emerged as Chandika from an eyebrow
of goddess Ambika and was assigned the task to eliminate the
demons. Chandika destroyed these two demons and presented
their heads in front of Ambika. Pleased with the act of Chamunda
the goddess Ambika named the city as Chamunda, and since
then, the temple Chamunda Devi is worshipped with grace and
faith.

Thus, all these legends associated with different
manifestations of the goddess Ambika continue to remind
the generation, and the philosophy of Shakti. It is said that
in the beginning there was the cosmic being as the *atman*
(soul) in human form, who could never feel happy, i.e., enjoy

himself through any process of self-realisation, for he was all alone. So, he desired to be second to him. His being was something like a neutral point where the ultimate principles of the male and the female lay unified in a deep embrace, as it were. This unified being divided himself into two: as the male and the female, which formed the first pair, and the pairs of the universe are said to be replicas of this original pair. This information is contained in *Brihadaranyaka Upanishad*, which has been reproduced in the *Puranas*, in the *Tantras* as also in the later Buddhist and Vaishnava Sahajiya schools, in which the idea of Shakti played an important part.

In Jainism, goddesses were first introduced as attendant deities of the twenty-four liberators known as *Jinas*. Of these, Ambika is associated with the mango tree and its fruit is always portrayed with one or both of her sons. She is worshipped on behalf of mothers and infants.

Damayanti

Damayanti, a character in Hindu mythology, was the princess of Vidarbha Kingdom, who married King Nala of Nishadha Kingdom. Their story finds mention in the epic *Mahabharata*. Damayanti's beauty and grace were so enchanting that even gods could not stop from admiring her. She fell in love with Nala simply from hearing about his virtues and accomplishments from a golden swan. When it was time for Damayanti to choose her husband at a *swayamvara*, gods and top princes as well as kings came to seek her hand. The story of Nala and Damayanti has inspired and has guided millions of women in India for thousands of years. It shows what sterling stuff women were made of in those days, never straying from their conjugal love even in the heaviest sorrows and misfortunes. Their tales of woe and ultimate triumph have added a new value to the age-old values of truth, chastity, and a host of human qualities that have transcended humanity to a divine status.

Nala was a brave, handsome young man well-versed in the science of war. He had an unusual skill in driving chariots. He held an exalted position among all the ruling princes. His only weakness was that he was fond of gambling. There was another king, Bhima, ruling over Vidarbha, who was known for his heroic deeds and his affection for his subjects. He had three sons and an exceedingly beautiful daughter, Damayanti.

King Nala had heard from various persons, who had been to the court of Bhima, about Princess Damayanti, eulogising her charming personality and virtues. On hearing them, Nala developed love for Damayanti in his mind. He could not resist himself and started living a lonely life in the garden attached to the royal apartments. One day, he saw there a flock of beautiful swans with golden wings and caught one of them. The swan somehow discovered the secret of his soul and said to him, 'O king, do not kill me. I shall go to Damayanti and speak to her of you that she will not care to marry any other man'. Thereupon, Nala released the bird and waited in breathless suspense for the result of its mission.

The whole flock alighted in the royal garden at Vidarbha where the princess was sporting with her friends. The young ladies were quite happy on seeing the golden-winged swans. One of the swans led Damayanti to a corner of the garden and addressed her like a human being. It suggested that Damayanti shall be blessed if she agrees to be Nala's wife. The princess felt happy and asked the swan to speak to Nala about her passionate love. When the swan reported this to the king, he made preparations for a *swayamvara-sabha*, an assembly of suitors, where the princess was to choose her own husband.

In *swayamvara-sabha*, when Nala glanced at Damayanti, his love for her became more intense, but he kept himself under control. Princess Damayanti came forward and asked him who he was. Nala revealed his identity and said that he had come to the place as messenger of the gods. He also told her that the gods wanted her to select one of them as her husband, but the choice was hers. Damayanti complimented the gods, but expressed her love to Nala and, in return, wanted to know whether Nala had similar sentiments for her. Nala asked Damayanti why she wanted him and what led her to brush aside the proposition of the gods.

Damayanti could not control her tears at this. She said that she had all respect for the gods but she had already selected Nala as her husband. This put Nala in an embarrassing situation. He asked for the fulfillment of his mission, which had brought him there. At this, Damayanti asked Nala to be present in the assembly along with Indra and the other gods and, in their presence, she would select him as her husband. In this way, nobody would blame him of his insincerity.

The assembly was held as per schedule. The princess was brought there. The kings were introduced to her one by one. Soon she found that five persons present there resembled Nala and four of them looked resplendent. They stood without touching the ground. The real Nala stood adjacent to them. Damayanti advanced gracefully, bowing to the kings as their names were proclaimed until the name of Nala was announced. She now stopped and looked up. Damayanti realised that the four celestial seekers had also assumed the form of Nala to seek her. Thereupon, she bowed to the gods with folded hands and said in trepidation, 'From the moment, I listened to the swan, I have accepted the King Nishadha as my husband.' She said that since she had taken a vow of adoring none other than Nala, she prayed to the gods to reveal Nala to her. In this way, she could now spot the real Nala and placed the garland around his neck.

Damayanti and Nala were happily married and had two children. Kali, who was one of the suitors for marriage to Damayanti, entered the palace as a servant, and waited for twelve long years spotting for the most little imperfection by which he could strike Nala. One day, Nala was in a rush to make his prayer. He made himself impure by not washing his feet, thereby allowing Kali to bewitch his soul.

After sometime, King Nala, under the influence of Goddess Kali, the personification of *Kali Yuga*, was lured to play dice with his wicked brother Pushkara. He gambled away almost the whole of his wealth and kingdom. It hurt the feelings of Damayanti, but she maintained her fortitude. Nala's brother wanted him now to put Damayanti at stake since Nala was not left with anything else. This greatly angered Nala, and he immediately left the place with only cloth on his person. Damayanti, dressed in one piece of cloth, followed him.

The royal couple was now penniless. They were hungry for three consecutive days, but nobody offered them food and water. They went to the forest. Nala came across some birds with wings shining like gold. He was virtually mad with hunger and with a desire to possess something valuable, took away his only cloth and threw it over the birds. The birds flew and Nala became naked and started trembling. Damayanti offered Nala half of her own cloth and consoled him. Nala wanted Damayanti to go to her father's kingdom, but Damayanti was reluctant to desert Nala. Nala started worrying for Damayanti and, obscured by Kali, resolved to abandon her in order to protect her from his bad luck.

The couple shared the same cloth and lay together. Damayanti felt tired and she fell fast asleep. Nala thought that if Damayanti is left on her own she would ultimately find her father's home and would live there comfortably. Her reunion with her children would help her to bear the pangs of separation from him. Kali forced Nala to abandon Damayanti. But how could he go away naked. He could not tear the piece of cloth, which he shared with his wife, fearing that it might wake her. He glanced at a sword nearby. He picked it and severed the garment in two and ran away leaving his wife in that forest. But his love for her resisted him, and he returned again and again to have a last glimpse of his wife. When Damayanti woke up, she found herself alone in that forest. A number of plans flashed in the mind of Nala. He was not in favour of seeing his queen in such a pitiable condition. When Damayanti woke up, not finding her husband nearby she cried loudly and even became unconscious sometime. But she never blamed her husband.

Damayanti found herself alone in the forest and enacted a curse against those who had caused the downfall of her husband. Nala encountered one misfortune after the other. He lost his strength. In the meantime, Nala rescued a Snake King Naga Karkotaka from fire. As a result, Naga Karkotaka bit him in rewards. As Nala sought for an explanation, Naga Karkotaka told Nala that the poison would only take effect when it was perfect. Nala survived the bite, but the venom turned him into an unrecognisable dwarf. He assumed the name of Bahuka and served as a charioteer to the King Rituparna of Ayodhya. Damayanti started walking and stumbled on a peaceful hermitage. There she saw sages sitting in their rustic cottages. They welcomed her like a daughter and wanted her to take rest. They offered her some refreshment. She narrated her woeful tale to them, saying that if she is not able to find Nala she would give up her own life. Her lamentations stirred the hearts of the ascetics. The holy persons predicted that she would soon join her husband, and the couple would lead a happy life. The words of the ascetics assuaged her bruised feelings. She regained her strength, and for a moment, she was lost in thinking. When she opened her eyes, the ascetics were not there.

While half-clad, pale, and looking like a skeleton, Damayanti met a caravan of merchants resting near a ford. They permitted her to travel with them to their destination, Chedi. At night, a herd of wild elephants came and killed some of the merchants. With superstitious feelings, the survivors blamed Damayanti for the misfortune they had faced. She ran away to the forest and reached a wide road, entered Chedi, and stood by the palace gate. The queen of Chedi saw her from the terrace and sent her nurse to bring her. Damayanti narrated her poignant tale to the queen without disclosing her identity, but did not like to send a message to her father.

Nala started working under Rituparna, king of Ayodhya, driving his chariot. There his own driver Varshneya had been employed. Damayanti's father, Bhima, sent Brahmana messengers all around to find out the whereabouts of Damayanti and Nala. One of the messengers spotted Damayanti in Chedi with Princess Sunanda. The princess was happy to find that she had given shelter to the daughter of her sister, the queen of Vidarbha. But Damayanti could no longer stay away from her beloved children. Therefore, she took leave and left to join them. She was quite happy to meet them in her father's house. There she requested her father to trace her husband. Damayanti started thinking that the only way Nala would come back would be the fear that she would not be her wife anymore. That is why she requested a second *swayamvara*. She was still of irresistible beauty that many kings wanted to attend. Nala's master also wanted to go to the *swayamvara*, and Nala accompanied him. On their journey to the *swayamvara*, the king instructed the dwarf in the techniques of gambling.

Damayanti asked the messengers to repeat a few couplets while searching for her husband. In the couplets, she complained to her husband that he had cheated her by cutting away half of her cloth and left his devoted wife while she was asleep. In the couplets, she also requested Nala to have pity on her and join her. Though Damayanti suffered, yet she remained true to her lord.

After a long time, a Brahmana, named Parnada, returned home with the news that only one person had responded to the recitation of his couplets, but that person was dwarf. The dwarf, Damayanti believed, could be Nala. She asked the person to go to Ayodhya and tell King Rituparna that Damayanti, not knowing where Nala was, had decided to hold a marriage assembly the next morning, and that kings and princes were coming there. This was a clever ruse on the part of Damayanti to invite Nala from Ayodhya. Rituparna resolved to start immediately with his driver hoping to win the hand of Damayanti. Bahuka was quite fast in driving the chariot. On their journey to the *swayamvara*, the king, who himself was adept in the game of dice, instructed the dwarf in the techniques of gambling. When King Rituparna revealed to him the supreme skill of controlling the dice, the poison finally takes effect and Bahuka vomited Kali from his body and imprisoned him temporarily in a tree.

When the king of Ayodhya arrived at Vidarbha, he was surprised to see no preparations for the marriage assembly. Damayanti felt convinced that the dwarf was Nala because of the flavour of a dish that he cooked for her, and was happy to see him there. She sent her children to him. Nala embraced them. Nala also looked different having been subjected to extreme penury.

Bahuka, the charioteer, was persuaded to be brought to the apartment where Damayanti presented herself as a thin and pale, dressed only in half a piece of cloth, with true love shining through her eyes. Damayanti was persuaded that the dwarf was Nala because of the flavour of a dish that he cooked for her. The two were reunited and Nala was transformed from being a dwarf into his familiar form. He used the knowledge of gambling he had gained in order to regain everything he had lost. Nala's heart was nearly broken, but he checked himself. Damayanti felt choked with tears. Both of them exchanged their feelings. She forgave him for having abandoning her in the forest, and he forgave her for having organised another *swayamvara*. Nala repented over his behaviour in deserting her.

Nala put on a magic garment and regained his radiant form. The couple was now reunited. They embraced each other. Nala went to his brother and challenged him in the game of dice.

Nala now won every time. He could have inflicted the cruellest punishment on his brother, but he pardoned him. Damayanti now occupied the throne along with her husband. They lived happily ever after. Their virtues were sung by the court minstrels. Until now, the couple is remembered for their faithful love and constancy.

Devahuti

The creator of this Universe, Lord Brahma realised that for the world to be populated he had to create a race that would itself procreate. Hence, he created the first man and first woman. The first man was Swayambhav Manu. Swayambhav means self-formed, implying that he was not born in the normal way. Manu means man. The first woman was Shatrupa, which means 'very beautiful'. In the *Bhagavata Purana* the primeval king of the human race, and Shatrupa, Lord Brahma's first female creation Swayambhav Manu and Shatrupa then united in a sexual relationship and became the progenitors of the human race.

Swayambhav Manu and Shatrupa had five children. Three were daughters named Akruti, Devahuti and Prasuti, and two sons named Priyavrata and Uttanapada. The three daughters were married to three of the persons created by Brahma. Akruti was married to sage Ruchi, Devahuti to sage Kardam, and Prasuti to Daksha.

The marriage of Devahuti and Kardam is described in detail in canto 3, chapters 21 and 22 of the *Srimad Bhagavata Purana*. Devahuti had, from her very birth, all the features of yoga natural in her. When she grew up, she heard of Prajapati Kardam's character and attainments as a great sage. She was then determined to have him as her husband. On the other hand, Brahma instructed Kardam, who he had created from his shadow, to get children. Kardam then prayed to Vishnu on the banks of the Lake Bindu Sarovar for a suitable bride. Kardam was anxious to have a suitable wife so that by having sons he might relieve himself of the obligations to his *pitris* (manes). For this purpose, he worshipped Vishnu who assured Kardam that he would marry Devahuti, daughter of Swayambhav Manu and have him a son under the name of Kapila.

Vishnu appeared before the sage in all his glory and said, 'Swayambhav Manu, the emperor of the world, and his wife Shatrupa will approach you with the proposal of marriage of his daughter Devahuti.' Vishnu described Devahuti as a beautiful maiden who possessed qualities suitable for being Kardam's wife. Vishnu asked Kardam to accept her. Vishnu told Kardam that from the seeds sown in her by him, she would bear nine daughters, and Kardam should give these daughters in marriages to the holy sages for further procreation of the human race, thereby fulfilling the desires of his father, Brahma.

As foretold by Vishnu, Swayambhav Manu, Shatrupa and Devahuti arrived at the ashram of sage Kardam on their golden chariot. The emperor bowed down before the sage, and, in turn, the sage welcomed him as befitting a monarch. Then Kardam said to Manu, 'Despite your unending duties of protecting the righteous and vanquishing the unrighteous you have taken the time to come here. Please tell me what is your desire and it will be done.'

Manu, in turn, praised all Brahmins in general and sage Kardam in particular. He then said, 'My daughter Devahuti has reached a marriageable age and like all fathers I am too concerned about her future. Sage Narada described to her your qualities, and she fell in love with you. Since you have not taken the vow of celibacy, I am requesting you to accept her as your wife.'

The sage Kardam accepted the proposal. The luster emanating from Devahuti's body outshined her ornaments. Kardam told Manu that the Gandharva, Vishwavasu, was 'so smitten by her when he saw her playing in your palace that he fell down and apart from the fact that Devahuti is your daughter, she is worthy bride in her own right'. However, he agreed on one condition that he would live with her only till her conception, after which he would resume his life of austerities. Devahuti agreed to this. After getting the consent of Kardam, Swayambhav Manu performed the marriage ceremony according to Vedic rites and returned to his capital at Barhishmati with his wife. This story appears in the *Bhagavata Purana* (3, 21–33).

For many years, Devahuti served her husband with devotion and care. For a pretty long time, she continued her vigilant and selfless service. Though she was a princess, she easily adjusted to the life of the hermitage. She spent all her spare time observing religious rituals and soon her body lost its voluptuousness and became lean and emaciated. She wished to win her husband's blessings by rendering whole-hearted service to him, and in attending upon him she totally shunned pride, hatred, avarice and other passions, and had no regard for her own body.

Once Kardam noticed her weak condition and acknowledging all that she had done for him, he said that he would share his transcendental wisdom with her and furnish her with divine vision so that she might experience the celestial enjoyments she won by her service. Devahuti very bashfully replied that time for sharing of the minds would come. The union of the bodies was also essential, after all the purpose of their marriage was to further the human race. She requested her husband to fulfil this duty as he had been fulfilling all others.

Using his yogic powers, Kardam created a seven-story flying palace. It was bedecked with jewels and flowers alike and possessed every comfort that could be required to create a romantic atmosphere conducive for sexual union. The palace had pleasure gardens with exotic flowers and birds, resting chambers that would vanquish fatigue in a second and bedrooms that would bring out feelings of love. Kardam also created a thousand maidservants who bathed Devahuti in the magical waters of Bindu Sarovar and thereafter dressed and adorned her so beautifully that she would have been able to charm Kama Deva himself if he had been present.

In the flying palace, Kardam and Devahuti travelled to all the romantic places in the world, including the valley of Mount Meru and the chores of Manasarovar Lake. They were now completely ready for producing children. The couple returned to their hermitage. Kardam split himself into nine personalities and impregnated his wife nine times so that she gave birth to nine daughters.

Devahuti remembered the condition that Kardam had placed before her marriage. Once he had fulfilled his obligation of siring children, he would forsake family life and become an ascetic. When, after this, Kardam prepared to renounce all worldly attachments, Devahuti approached him with an afflicted mind and said, 'Your revered self has performed for me all that was promised; yet you should be pleased to grant immunity from fear to me who have sought your protection. O Brahman, your daughters will have to approach you for worthy husbands, and there should be some male offspring to console me after you have retired to the forest. There is no use of speaking about this for a long period of time, my lord, which I have passed with attachment to objects of the senses giving up the Supreme Soul. Being addicted to objects of the senses, I associated myself with you without knowing the final truth from you; yet, let this be for my immunity from fear. Association, when formed with the wicked through imprudence, becomes the cause of rebirths, but the same is conducive to freedom from attachment if it is made with the good. One, whose work here is meant neither for the attainment of religious merit (*dharma*) nor for creating indifference or rendering service to the Lord is as good as dead, even though one may be living. Surely, I have been beguiled by the magic power of your revered self, since I felt no desire for freedom from bondage even after having you, the bestower of final release.'

Kardam assuaged Devahuti's fears, saying that the time for him to leave her had not come. Vishnu, the Supreme God, had given him a boon that he would be born as their son. He declared that Devahuti's womb is truly sacred. Many years later, Devahuti conceived again. The heavens rejoiced at this event, and the *Devas* showered petals on Devahuti.

Brahma came to Kardam's hermitage with nine sages that he had earlier created using his mental powers. Nine daughters of Devahuti were now noble. Brahma asked Kardam to give them away to the nine sages. According to Brahma's wishes, Kala was married to sage Marichi, Anuya to sage Atri, Shradha to sage Angiras, Harirbhu to sage Plulastya, Gati to sage Pulaha, Kriya to sage Kratu, Khyati to sage Bhrigu, Shanti to sage Atharya and Arundhati to sage Vashishtha. Brahma then told Kardam and Devahuti that the manifestation of Vishnu in Devahuti's womb is to be named Kapila. And when he grows up, Kapila will be a renowned sage, and will spread the name of his parents as well. Kardam did not treat the baby boy as his son but as the father of the universe.

Lord Kapila became the fifth incarnation, the foremost among perfected beings. Devahuti had worshipped Vishnu for a long time, after which the deity was pleased to be born in Devahuti's womb as Kapila. Kardam left for the forest. After this, Kapila began to live with his mother for doing good to her. One day, Devahuti said to Kapila, 'O great one, I have become very much disgusted with the thirst of my wicked organs of sense, by going to satisfy which I have entered into blinding darkness. O Almighty one, today, through thy favour I have received thee, after a number of births, as an excellent eye that takes me through that blinding darkness that is difficult to cross. Thou who art said to be the pre-eminent and glorious Lord of all beings, art, like the sun that has risen, the eye of the world blinded by darkness. Now, O Lord, be pleased to remove my infatuation, which is a false idea of "I", "mine", etc., created by thee with respect to this body. I betake myself to thee, who deserved to be approached for protection and are an axe to the tree of rebirths of myself and my dependants. With a desire to know of *Prakriti* and *Purusha*, I bow down to thee, the best of the knower's of the religion of the good.'

By this time, Kapila attained the stature of Maharishi Kapila, a Vedic sage, traditionally considered to be the original proponent of the *Sankhya* system of philosophy and the foremost among the perfected beings. When Maharishi Kapila came to know of his mother's sincere and honest wish, he spoke out *Sankhya-yoga* with an elaborate discourse on *bhakti* (devotion). He instructed his mother, Devahuti, in the philosophy of yoga. He also gave great expositions to his mother on the science of devotional service to the Supreme Lord to enable her to achieve both liberation (*moksha*) and pure love of God. In this way, Devahuti became cleansed of all material tendencies and achieved liberation. The spiritual knowledge she acquired is provided in detail in *Srimad Bhagavatnam*. Some of its portions are as follows:

My appearance in this world is especially to explain the philosophy of Sankhya, which is highly esteemed for self-realisation by those desiring freedom from the entanglement of unnecessary material desires. This path of self-realisation, which is difficult to understand, has now been lost in the course of time. Please know that I have assumed this body of Kapila to introduce and explain this philosophy to human society again. (3.24, 36–37).

When one is completely cleansed of the impurities of lust and greed produced from the false identification of the body as "I" and bodily possessions as "mine", one's mind becomes purified. In that pure state he transcends the stage of so-called material happiness and distress. (3.25, 160).

The Supreme personality of godhead is the Supreme Soul, and He has no beginning. He is transcendental to the material modes of nature and beyond the existence of this material world. He is perceivable everywhere because He is self-effulgent, and by His devotees one should meditate on the eternal form of the Lord until the mind becomes fixed. (3.28, 18).

He added at the end that this *Sankhya-yoga* had been declared by him in ancient times to the inquisitive sages, and that by it people could realise the *Purusha* (Supreme Being) by getting out of the influence of *Prakriti* (nature).

When Kapila was explaining his metaphysical and philosophical views, Devahuti put to him searching questions, which amply testify to her uncommon interest and wisdom. Kapila's instructions enlightened Devahuti, who, thus, became a *Brahmavadini*, an expounder of Brahman, in the true sense of the term and was, through absolute meditation, absorbed into the Supreme Spirit.

Devahuti's son, Maharishi Kapila, became a major figure in the story associated with the Hindu holiday of Makar Sankranti, about bringing down the River Ganges from heaven, which involves King Sagar of Ayodhya, an ancestor of Rama. King Sagar had performed the *Ashwamedha* sacrifice ninety nine times. Each time a horse was sent around the earth, Indra, the king of the heaven, grew jealous and kidnapped the horse, hiding it in the hermitage of Kapila Muni during the hundredth sacrifice. The sixty thousand sons of Sagar found the horse, and, believing Kapila to be the abductor assaulted him. Kapila turned the assailants to ashes. Anshuman, a grandson of King Sagar, son of Asamanjas, the wicked son of King Sagar, came to Kapila begging him to redeem the souls of the sixty thousand sons. Kapila replied that only if the Ganges descended from heaven and touched the ashes of the sixty thousand sons would they be redeemed.

Draupadi

The marriage of Draupadi with five Pandava brothers, as depicted in the epic *Mahabharata*, is perhaps the single instance of polyandry in Indian history. The Indo-Aryan texts almost never mention or allow polyandry, although polygamy had been common among men of higher social ranks. Draupadi is regarded by most Hindus as an example of *bhakti* (devotion) to God. She shows utmost faith in Lord Krishna. And he protects her, showing that our faith in God always pays. She is the embodiment of courage, fortitude, sense and sensibility, and even pride and prejudice. The very circumstances of her birth made it abundantly clear that she had come to this world to fulfil a great destiny.

King Drupada of Panchala had been defeated by the Pandava Prince Arjuna on behalf of Drona, who subsequently took half his kingdom to humiliate him. To gain revenge on Drona, he performed a fire sacrifice (*yajna*) to obtain a son who could kill him. Draupadi emerged as a beautiful dark-skinned young woman, with her brother Drishtadyumna from the sacrificial fire. She was named 'Krishna' at this time for her complexion.

Drupada intended that Arjuna alone win the hand of his daughter, Draupadi. When she came of age, her father arranged a *swayamvara-sabha* (marriage assembly) in order that she might have the opportunity of selecting her own husband. Upon hearing of the Pandavas' supposed death at Varanavata he announced the setting up of *swayamvara* for Draupadi, intending to bring Arjuna out into the open. A number of princes and kings, known for bravery and skill in archery were present there. They included Kaurava brothers as well. Pandava brothers entered the assembly in the guise of Brahmins, as they were not supposed to disclose themselves being in exile. In that great assembly, the foremost heroes of India, Arjuna, showed his prowess in archery by piercing with arrow the eye of a moving fish on a high pole, looking into the fish's image in a cauldron of oil below, and won Draupadi as his bride.

While in exile, Kunti, mother of the Pandavas, often advised her sons that they were to share everything they had or obtained through *bhiksha*, i.e., alms equally amongst themselves. Upon returning home with Draupadi, after winning her hand in *swayamvara*, Bhima addressed his mother first, 'Look mother,

I have brought *bhiksha* (alms)!' Kunti, unmindful of what Bhima was referring to, unassumingly asked her son to share whatever it was with his brothers. Thus, in order to obey their mother's order all five brothers accepted Draupadi as their wife, without taking her consent. Later, when Yudhisthira became the king of Hastinapura at the end of the war, Draupadi became his queen. She is sometimes called Krsna (Krishna), which means dark-complexioned. She is also known as Panchali (literally the one from the kingdom of Panchala).

When sage Vyasa visited the family, he explained to Draupadi that her unique position as the wife of five brothers had resulted from a certain incident in her previous birth. She had in that lifetime prayed to Lord Shiva to grant her a husband with five desired qualities. Lord Shiva, pleased with her devotion, had told her that it was very difficult to get a husband with all five qualities that she desired. But she stuck to her ground and asked for the same. Then Lord Shiva granted her wish, saying that she would get the same in her next birth. Hence, Draupadi was married to five brothers; each of them represented a given quality.

Yudhisthira and his four brothers were the rulers of Indraprastha under the sovereignty of King Dhritarashtra. Dhritarashtra's son Duryodhana, who resided in the capital of the empire Hastinapur, was always jealous of his cousins, and the wealth they had acquired by building Indraprastha. To take revenge on the Pandavas, his uncle Shakuni treacherously came up with a plan and together with his brothers, his friend Karna, and maternal uncle Shakuni, he conspired to call the Pandavas at Hastinapur to win their kingdoms in gambling. Shakuni was skilled at winning by unfair means. The idea was that Shakuni would play against Yudhisthira and win at the gambling table what was impossible to win at the battlefield.

As the game proceeded, Yudhisthira, lost all his wealth and kingdom one by one. Having lost all material wealth, he went on to put his brothers at stake one by one and lost them too. Ultimately, he put himself at stake, and lost again. All the Pandavas were now the servants of Kauravas. But for the villain Shakuni, the humiliation of Pandavas was not complete. Yudhisthira now trapped into Shakuni's machinations and to the horror of everybody present lost even Draupadi as a bet for the next round. But, Bhishma and Guru Dronacharya opposed this move, recalling that a queen being a woman cannot be put at stake. However, Yudhisthira ignored their call and put her at stake much to the ire of Bhishma, who, in his frustration, broke his chair. Shakuni rolled the dice and gleefully shouted, 'Look, I have won'. Duryodhana commanded his younger brother Dushasana to forcefully bring Draupadi into the forum. Dushasana barged into the living quarters of Draupadi, who was menstruating at that time, and hence, 'clad in only one piece of attire'. Dushasana grabbed her by the hair and brought her into the court, dragging her by the hair.

Unable to withstand the distress of his wife, an emotional Bhima threatened to burn up Yudhisthira's hands with which he placed Draupadi on stake, but Arjuna stopped him. Now, in an emotional appeal to the elders present in the forum, Draupadi repeatedly questioned the legality of the right of Yudhisthira to place her at stake when he himself had lost his freedom, and as a consequence did not possess any property in the first place. Everybody remained dumbfounded. Bhishma, the patriarch of the Kaurava family and a formidable warrior had only this explanation to offer to Draupadi: 'The course of morality is subtle and even the illustrious wise in this world fail to always understand it.' Duryodhana now commanded the Pandavas to strip themselves in the manner of *dasa*. They obeyed by stripping off their upper garments.

Then Kauravas demanded the same from Draupadi who refused. Then to the horror of everybody present, Dushasana tried to strip Draupadi of her sari. Seeing her husbands unable or unwilling to help her, Draupadi prayed to Lord Krishna to protect her. A miracle occurred. As Dushasana unwrapped layers and layers of Draupadi's sari, her sari kept getting extended. This miracle is attributed to the help extended by Lord Krishna. Bhima was furious at Dushasana and said, 'I Bhim, Pandu's son vows until I tear open Dushasana's chest and drink his blood, I will not show my face to my ancestors.' Finally, a tired Dushasana backed off without being able to strip Draupadi.

Krishna treated Draupadi as his sister, pledged his friendship to Draupadi, and vowed to show the world the greatest example of friendship. He protected her whenever she asked him for help. As per Narada and Vayu Puranas, Draupadi was an incarnation of Goddesses Shyamala (wife of Dharma), Bharati (wife of Vayu), Sachi (wife of Indra), Usha (wife of Ashwinis), and hence married their earthly counterparts in the form of the five Pandavas. Enraged at a jest by Parvati, Shyamala, Sachi, and Usha, Brahma cursed them for human birth. Parvati thought of the solution wherein they will be born as one woman, Draupadi, and hence, share the earthly body for a smaller period of time. They requested Bharati to be with them in their human birth. Draupadi's characteristic fight against injustice reflects Parvati or her Shakti and Kali, inhabiting Draupadi's mortal flesh at times. At other times, Draupadi was docile and even waited to be rescued showing the qualities of other goddesses like Sachi and Usha. At other times, she showed astuteness in hiding their true identity and asking *Vayu-putra* Bhima to kill the evil Keechaka like Goddess Bharati would. Draupadi was also an incarnation of Goddess Shree or Wealth who was the joint wife of five Indras, the five Pandavas. She was to be born several times for imprisoning the Indras. First, as Vedavati who cursed Ravana (who is another goddess avatar Swaha, wife to Agni). She then was born as Maya-Sita, especially to take revenge on Ravana while Agni hid the real Sita. Third one was partial either Damayanti (whose husband Nala was equivalent to Dharma, Vayu, Indra just like the Pandavas) and her daughter Nalayani. She married sage Mudgala.

Krishna helped Draupadi because she prayed with utmost devotion. When Krishna had cut his finger on the Sudarshan Chakra, she bound it with her sari, this act being the origin of *Rakhi*. Another story of the origin of *Rakhi* is Sachi tying a thread on Indra. Krishna is also the one who opposed her marriage to Karna and promoted her marriage to Arjuna. In the Mahabharata war that ensued none of Draupadi's children survived the end of the epic. Parikshit, grandson of Subhadra and Arjuna, remained the sole Pandava descendent who survived at the end of *Mahabharata*.

Draupadi is the central figure in the epic *Mahabharata*. Her beauty was indescribable, and her body emitted the fragrance of a blue lotus. She was a veritable goddess in human form. As a wife, Draupadi became the ideal mistress of the household when Yudhisthira was installed as king of Indraprastha (modern Delhi). Yudhisthira performed a great sacrifice, known as

Rajasuya in which kings from different parts of India participated and rendered homage to him as the paramount overlord. The ceremony lasted for a number of days, and the Kaurava brothers also joined the ceremony. Duryodhana became quite jealous on seeing the immense prosperity of the Pandavas and returned to Hastinapura with a heavy heart. He related to his father how Draupadi had supervised the feeding of all alike, from the highest to the lowest, herself remaining without food till everybody was fed and satisfied.

Draupadi was the embodiment of courage and a sense of dignity. When Yudhisthira lost her in a game of dice, and Dushasana, brother of Duryodhana, heaped all sorts of insults upon her in the open assembly, she turned around to the members present and asked for protection and justice. Finding everybody silent, she rebuked the open assembly, saying that sense of justice had disappeared from India and that the members of the warrior caste had forgotten their duties. When Dushasana tried to disrobe her in front of everyone present in the assembly, she accused him of savage conduct. As a last resource, she made a passionate appeal to the elders in the assembly to come to her rescue. But even Bhishma, the noblest man and greatest warrior of the age, proved helpless. The only person who raised a protest was Vidura who earnestly exhorted everybody present to express his disapproval of the heinous conduct of Dushasana. Bhima then announced that Dushasana would have to pay dearly for his heinous act. Ultimately, Lord Krishna, to whom she was quite devoted, came to her rescue, though he himself was present in Dwarka at that time. As explained above, Lord Krishna provided her an endless supply of cloth to her sari so that it never ended, and she was always covered and not dishonoured in such a way.

Yet, another episode that shows Draupadi as a devotee of Lord Krishna was when Durvasa Muni, who was known for his quick anger, suddenly decided to drop in on the Pandava camp along with his many thousands of disciples. He wanted something to eat for himself and his followers. But the Pandavas had just eaten, and there was nothing more to prepare. Lord Krishna asked for whatever remnant grains were left in the pot. Being the Supreme Lord, if he was satisfied, everyone would be satisfied. Therefore, he took what few grains were there, and when Durvasa Muni arrived, they were all so full that they no longer wanted anything to eat, and thus left peacefully.

Draupadi proved an ideal wife. Like Sita, she proved to be a true companion for her husbands. When Pandava brothers were exiled, Draupadi accompanied them to the forest, leaving aside all sorts of comforts she had so far been enjoying first as a princess and later as a queen, though nursing her grief but with great fortitude. She had been getting up early in the morning before anyone else, tolerated hunger and thirst, and went to bed after the others. She also gave birth to five sons, all of whom were killed by the wicked Ashwathama. But, since he was the son of the family guru, and she had such respect for the gurus, she forgave him.

Once, when Krishna had been to the forest to enquire about the condition of Pandava brothers, Draupadi related with tears in her eyes that she could not forget for a moment that a woman of her status could be so openly humiliated in the presence of the Pandavas. Krishna at once assured her that the wives of the Kauravas would have to weep in the same manner as she was doing on that day. Krishna also assured her that she would ultimately become an empress, and therefore, she was not to worry. These words of Krishna soothed her injured feelings. At one time, she deliberated the subject of dharma with Yudhisthira and succeeded in proving his thesis that dharma was an all-pervading law in the universe, and its pursuit was never fruitless. He asked her to banish all her doubts regarding the triumph of dharma. When Satyabhama, Krishna's wife, asked Draupadi how she could manage her household affairs with great skill, and how could she win the confidence, love, and respect of the Pandava brothers, her discourse on the duties and responsibilities of the wife on this occasion is one of the important chapters of the *Mahabharata.*

Draupadi's patience and endurance became manifest especially when during the last year of her sojourn in the forest, and when Pandava brothers were expected to remain incognito. They lived in the house of Virata, king of Matsya country, each one of them in disguise. She had to work there as a maidservant and as an escort of the queen. What an irony of life that the lady who was once a queen herself had to serve as a maidservant. She voluntarily accepted this position and handled it with great dexterity, never letting anybody know of her identity. She had to endure all kinds of trials and tribulations for one year, though she had to hear insults from the commander-in-chief, Kichaka. At one stage, she had the audacity to say that the law of the jungle prevailed in the kingdom of Virata. She also declared that the king was unworthy of his royal seat and that even the members of the court were not true to their dharma, inasmuch as they worshipped such an incompetent king. She even hinted that members of the assembly should rise against the king and depose him. However, there was a blessing in disguise and the stay of Pandava brothers in the house of Virata paved the way for amicable relationship between the King Virata and Pandava brothers through marriage alliance of Abhimanyu, the son of Arjuna, and Uttara, the daughter of Virata.

Draupadi also proved to be a unique life companion, helpmate, and life partner. In her last phase of life, she accompanied Pandava brothers in the final great journey. The only pilgrim in the group who could reach the goal was Yudhisthira, who was a paradigm of unflinching moral virtues. He did not look behind, nor did he turn either to the left or to the right, but moved straight on. But, in spite of her failings, Draupadi remained a unique type of woman, not merely a fond and devoted wife, but a true helpmate and partner in life's affairs. When the Pandavas had reached the end of their lives and were setting out to ascend to heaven by climbing up on the mountains, she was the last in line. But she was the first to fall, and thus rise to heaven after her death. Her dedication and devotion made her one of the great personalities of Vedic culture. She was perhaps the best illustration of Kalidasa's famous verse, 'A good housewife, wise counsellor, dear companion, and a beloved pupil in the cultivation of the fine arts.'

Finally, Draupadi has been shown in the epic *Mahabharata* as a unique character showing great courage, endurance, and firm in her resolve even if she had to encounter all sorts of trials and tribulations. With a view to fulfil her vow (a promise to herself to tie her untied hair after washing them with the blood of Dushasana) and to punish all those who had disgraced her and perpetrated offence against her, she kept ablaze the fire of revenge burning in her heart into the hearts and minds of Pandavas. She was the very embodiment of *shree* or good fortune in the house of the Pandavas. No doubt, she was occasionally subject to moods of indignation, but the loftiness of her soul, her unfailing courage in the face of disasters, her spirit of self-sacrifice, and, above all, her moral earnestness and spiritual integrity have shed a luster on the ideals of womanhood in ancient India. Her character has been woven by Maharishi Krishna Dwaipayana with great skill. The very circumstances of her birth made it abundantly clear that she was destined to fulfil a significant role. Thus, the refulgence of Draupadi's lustrous prototype of womanhood shall always be a source of inspiration for the women of India.

Gargi

Saraswati as the goddess of learning in Hindu mythology is indicative of the fact that women in India have never been far behind men in learning and scholarship. In the Vedic age, women enjoyed equal opportunities for education and work. They were eligible for *upanayana* or initiation and *brahmacharya* or study of Brahma-knowledge. The list of great Vedic teachers to whom tribute of respect had to be paid at the time of Brahmayajna includes the names of some ladies like Gargi Vachaknavi, Vadava Pratitheyi, and Sulabha Maitreyi. Such women made great strides in establishing the foundation of *Sanatan Dharma* or eternal religion and Vedic culture. They serve as fine examples of historical importance that have been the basis for inspiration to both men and women for centuries. Out of these women seers, Gargi had the profound knowledge of spiritual science.

Gargi Vachaknavi was an ancient Indian female philosopher, daughter of sage Vachaknu, and born in the family of Garga. She is mentioned in the sixth and the eighth Brahmana of Brahmayajna Upanishad, where the *Brahmayajna*, a philosophic congress organised by King Janaka of Videha is described when she challenged the sage Yajnavalkya with perturbing questions on the *atman* (soul). In Vedic literature, she is honoured as one of the great natural philosophers. Gargi composed several hymns that questioned the origin of all existence. *Yogayajnavalkya Samhita*, a classical text on yoga, is a dialogue between sage Yajnavalkya and Gargi. She was one of the Navaratnas in the court of King Janaka of Mithila.

Gargi was the wise and learned daughter of the sage Vachaknu and was also called Vachaknvi. She was also known as Brahmavadini because of her knowledge of *Brahma-vidya*. As she was born in the line of the Garga Gotra or family line, she was also called Gargi, a name by which she became well known. Gargi was that special lady who having awakened her *Kundalini* indulged herself in the famous dialogues with Pundit Mandan Mishra on the topic of sex. Gargi finally defeated Pundit Mandan Mishra for she was a truly God realised soul. It is said that *Kundalini* awakening is better possible in a man. It is not something that can be taught from books. It only comes from experience. One has to practice absolute celibacy and meditation. It is really frightening sometimes for the *Kundalini* awakening is accompanied by the shadow of a mammoth king cobra. Sage Jnanavalakya was that dominant force in the times of King Janaka that even before the contest among ten thousand *pundits* (learned persons) and sages gathered on stage had begun, sage Jnanavalakya ordered the prize money to be taken home. Sage Jnanavalakya was a truly God realised soul. His *Kundalini* had awakened fully, and he knew that none in the assembly had reached his level of spiritual attainment.

In the third chapter of *Brihadaranyaka Upanishad*, we find that King Janaka, the emperor of Videha, performed a sacrifice in which gifts were freely distributed among the priests. Brahmin scholars from the countries of Kuru and Panchala were assembled there. Emperor Janaka wished to know which of these Brahmins was the most erudite Vedic scholar. With this in view, he arranged a debate on spiritual sciences. He wanted to find out who was the person who knew best, the science of the Absolute. He offered one thousand decorated cows with horns plated with gold to such a person.

None of the local Brahmanas complied because they were afraid that they would have to prove their knowledge and may not be up to the task. However, sage Yajnavalkya told his disciple to take all the cows to his place, which started the debate. Thereupon, Yajnavalkya alone dared to claim this reward. After this, he was challenged and closely questioned on deep philosophical topics by eight celebrated scholars, including Gargi. So he confined thousand cows in a pen and fastened on the horns of each ten *padas* of gold. He then said to them: 'Venerable Brahmins, let him among you who is the best Vedic scholar drive these cows home.' None of the Brahmins dared. Then Yajnavalkya said to one of his pupils, 'Dear Samsrava, drive these cows home.' Taking the command from his guru, he drove the cows away.

The Brahmins were furious and challenged Yajnavalkya for a debate, relating the knowledge of Vedas. Many illustrious sages like Asvala, the priest of Janaka, Artabhaga, Bhujyu, Ushasta, and Uddalaka challenged him, and Yajnavalkya answered all their questions and defeated them in the debate.

Among them was a female sage Gargi, the daughter of Vachaknu, who was wise and well-versed in Vedas. Gargi asked many different and complex questions on the immortality of the soul, the arrangement of the universe, and many other topics. She questioned Yajnavalkya, if all this is pervaded by water, by what, pray, is water pervaded? Yajnavalkya replied, 'By what, pray, is air pervaded?' Gargi asked, 'By what is the sky pervaded?' The reply was 'By the world of the Gandharvas'. To this Gargi questioned, 'By what is the world of the Gandharvas pervaded?' The reply was 'By the world of the sun'. Gargi questioned, 'By what is the world of the sun pervaded?' The reply was 'By the world of the moon'. 'By what is the world of the moon pervaded?' was now Gargi's question. The reply was 'By the world of the stars'. To this she questioned, 'By what is the world of the stars pervaded?' The reply was 'By the world of the gods'. Gargi shot one more question, 'By what is the world of the gods pervaded?' The reply was 'By the world of Indra'.

Gargi was the only one among the sages and erudite scholars who had the courage to question Yajnavalkya twice, and it was on her advice that the Brahmanas acknowledged him to be the best knower of Brahman. Finally, Gargi herself bowed to the sage and proclaimed that there was no one else who was more greatly learned in the Vedic Shastras than Yajnavalkya. In this way, Gargi showed that in Vedic culture it was not unexpected for women to become greatly learned in the Vedic sciences, nor that they could not discuss topics with wise and kindly sages who also shared their knowledge with them. Thus, she had been a luminous example of women in the Vedic tradition.

Sulabha Maitreyi

Among the questions that Gargi posed, one was about the inner controller of all things. The sage replied:

He who is dwelling in all things and yet is other than all things, whose body all things are, who controls all things from within—He is your self, the inner ruler, immortal.

In the *Chhandogya Upanishad*, Gargi is stated to have described that 'the body is the support of deathless and the bodyless self.' She is also stated to have said here 'that which is the finest essence this whole world has that is its soul. That is reality. That is the *atman*.'

The individual soul has been termed as *Jiva*. It has four stages—awakening, dreaming, sleeping, and *turia*. The *Jiva* is enveloped in the five sheaths. They are named as *koshas* of the *Jiva* in *Taittirya Upanishad* as under—*annarasmaya*, *pranmaya*, *manomaya*, *vijnanamaya*, and *anandamaya*. These together constitute the empirical home of the *Jiva* in the end; the *Jiva* is liberated through the realisation of the reality. This soul is not born with the body and it does not even die. This unborn, constant, eternal, and primeval soul is not slain when the body is slain. On death, it migrates from one physical body and enters another, unless it attains release from the cycle of birth and death.

For her first question, Gargi riddles, 'That which is above heaven and below the earth, which is also between heaven and earth, which is the same through past, present, and future in which is that woven, warp and woof?' Yajnavalkya answers easily, 'in space'. For her second question, Gargi asks, 'In what is space itself woven, warp and woof?' Yajnavalkya's answers, 'The imperishable'.

When Gargi asks Yajnavalkya what pervades the world of the imperishable, he concedes and threatens, 'Do not question me beyond that. You may get crazy because you are questioning about a deity who cannot be known through mere reasoning.' One of the implications of Yajnavalkya's statement is that instead of conceding defeat in the debate, he is trying to dissuade Gargi from going into the construction of the belief system itself. If this assumption is correct, according to some scholars, Yajnavalkya might have acted because he felt that his own understanding and that of the Brahmanic religious doctrines also could not survive Gargi's critical examination.

His command, 'Do not question me beyond that', shows clearly the unequal power dynamics in the debate in which Gargi's role as questioner was further contingent on Yajnavalkya's willingness to participate in a discussion with her. Nevertheless, Gargi's questions reveal that she was rejecting the blind faith of the Vedas for her own spiritual journey.

Gargi's questions reveal a clear and poetic mind. She discusses profound concepts, such as the science and the unity of the material; and the non-material world and the illusion of time, in a way that is accessible to all. Astutely, she followed Yajnavalkya's simplistic answer to her first question with the same line of inquiry in her second question. She employed a feminine metaphor, like 'the womb', as a symbol for her discussion on the source of creation, for instance, 'in what is that woven, warp and woof?' 'Warp' suggests wrapping or creating an enclosed area while 'woof' alludes to the surrounding effect of sound. 'Woven' hinted at being covered by a garment as well as other domestic arts.

In this way, of all the seers in Indian mythology, Gargi appears to have been a more accomplished scholar, who questioned Yajnavalkya at great length upon the origin of all existence, until the great sage, perturbed by her questionings, exclaims, 'Ask not too much, Gargi, so that thy head may not fall off thy body. Truly, concerning divinity one must not ask too much. Thou dost ask too much. Gargi, ask not too much.' Thus silenced, she was, however, not subdued. Again, in an assembly of sages, she sought permission to ask two questions of the famous teacher, adding, 'Should he answer those, none of you can ever beat him in describing Brahman.' She then advanced towards Yajnavalkya fearlessly with the words, 'As a hero's son from Benaras or from Videha, strings the slackened bow and arises with two foe-piercing arrows in his hand, so I confront you with two questions. Answer me these.'

At the end of the highly philosophical dispute, she acknowledged her defeat, and very generously declared to the assembled sages, 'You should consider yourselves fortunate if you can get away from him with a salutation; never shall any of you beat him in describing Brahman.'

In contrast to the submissive, voiceless portrayal of women in the Vedic canon, as depicted in 'The Imperishable' in the *Brihadaranyaka Upanishads*, one gets quite a different representation of female spirituality in the voice of Gargi. Thus, Gargi Vachaknavi was a female philosopher who gained legendary repute for successfully debating prominent male philosophers during the Upanishadic period, including Yajnavalkya. She, like countless women, represented a challenge to males of her period. The challenge, as documented in the Vedas, has been critiqued upon by many European and Indian Vedic scholars, Hindu reformers, and writers.

Gargi's role as a woman in the Upanishads is an exceptional one. The unusual image of Gargi as an expert in spiritual discourse and, as represented in the Vedic text, is that of a woman who defies the construction of gender roles. She confronted Brahmanic patriarchy in a spiritual and intellectual struggle for her own empowerment. However, Gargi is mentioned only in a few places in the Upanishad texts. In 'The Imperishable', Gargi confidently warned Yajnavalkya, 'As a warrior from Kashi or Videha rises with a bow and arrow to fell the opponent. I rise to fell you with two questions.'

Gargi Vachaknavi stands out as the brightest luminary (*Brihadaranyaka Upanishad*, 3.6, 3.8) who took part in a public discussion on a philosophical subject with the great philosopher Yajnavalkya. She refused to take any share of the property of her husband, the great sage, when he was about to retire from home into the forest, and boldly asked him for instruction in the philosophic teachings about immortality of the soul. Above all, in her exchange of dialogue between the 'greatest' Upanishadic sages, Gargi represents a powerful icon countervailing the trend of devaluating women in Vedic texts while avoiding their glorification at the same time. Gargi's voice provides an exception of gender roles.

Maitreyi

M aitreyi, the woman seer and philosopher in Vedic times, was the wife of Yajnavalkya of Mithila, a legendary sage of Vedic India, credited with the authorship of the *Shatapatha Brahmana*, including the *Brihadaranyaka Upanishad*, *Yogayajnavalkya Samhita*, and the *Yajnavalkya Smrti*. Yajnavalkya was one of the greatest sages ever known. His precepts, as contained in the *Brihadaranyaka Upanishad*, stand foremost as the crest-jewel of the highest teachings on knowledge of Brahman. He has made important contributions to both philosophies, including the apophatic teaching of '*neti neti*' and to astronomy, describing the ninety five-year cycle to synchronise the motions of the sun and the moon. He was described as the greatest *bramajnani* by all the sages at a function organised by King Janaka.

Maitreyi is the wife of Yajnavalkya, who is also a major figure in the Upanishads. According to Indian tradition, he was the son of sage Devaraata and was the pupil of sage Vaishampayana. Once, Vaishampayana got angry with Yajnavalkya as the latter displayed too much sense of pride in being more competent than other students. The angry teacher asked Yajnavalkya to give back all the knowledge of *Yajurveda* he had taught him. As per the demands of his Guru, Yajnavalkya vomited all the knowledge that he acquired from his teacher in the form of eaten food. Other disciples of Vaishampayana took the form of patridge birds and consumed the vomited stuff because it was knowledge, and they were very eager to receive it. Yajnavalkya began to propitiate the Sun God, Surya, master of the Vedas for the purpose of acquiring the fresh Vedic portions not known to his preceptor, Vaishampayana. The Sun God, pleased with Yajnavalkya's penance, assumed the form of a horse and graced the sage with such fresh portions of the *Yajurveda*, which were not known to any other. This portion of the *Yajurveda* goes by the name of *Shukla Yajurveda* or *White-Yajurveda*, it being revealed by Sun, also known as *Vajasaneya Yajurveda*.

Yajnavalkya married two wives. One was Maitreyi and the other Katyayani. While Maitreyi was well-versed in the Hindu scriptures and was a '*Brahmavadini*', Katyayani was an ordinary woman. Maitreyi had a higher regard for spiritual knowledge and devotion to God than Katyayani. Once, at a contest, Yajnavalkya ordered the prize money to be taken home even before the contest amongst ten thousand *pundits* (intellectuals) among sages gathered on stage had begun. Maitreyi, his dutiful wife, was never after the mundane affairs of life. She contributed towards the enhancement of the image of Yajnavalkya's personality and the flowering of his spiritual thoughts. She yearned for gaining self-realisation within her lifetime. She knew well that her husband could impart her pearls of wisdom, gaining which she could get her kundalini awakened, and finally reach the stage of enlightenment.

The *Brihadaranyaka Upanishad*, the longest text of Hindu spirituality, describes the proceedings of a marvellous spiritual conference in which the great sage Yajnavalkya was locked in a debate with several sages on the other side. Suddenly, a woman sage, named Gargi Vachhavi, rose and said that if sage Yajnavalkya could answer her questions, all the other sages would accept his doctrines. All the sages present there accepted her as their spiritual leader and allowed her to represent them on their behalf. In the same text, Maitreyi, the wife of Yajnavalkya, motivated her husband to deliver a memorable sermon on the nature of God and soul. Modern India has honoured these illustrious women by founding colleges in New Delhi bearing their names.

The *Rigveda* contains about one thousand hymns of which about ten are accredited to Maitreyi. When the sage Yajnavalkya wanted to renounce the householder life to accept the *sannyasa* order of life, he expressed his intention to divide his possessions between his two wives. Maitreyi then questioned to herself what greater thing her husband must have found if he was willing to give up his present status in householder life. Surely, no one would give up his position unless he found something better. So, she asked her husband, 'Sir, if this whole earth, full of wealth, be mine, should I be immortal by it?' 'No', replied Yajnavalkya, 'like the life of rich people will be the life. But there is no hope of immortality by wealth.' Then Maitreyi said, 'What should I do with that which would not make me immortal?'

As soon as the idea of property arose, it appeared to have stirred up a brainwave in the mind of the wise Maitreyi. She queried, 'You speak of entering the fourth order of life, embracing a new perspective of living altogether, and, therefore, proposing to divide the property between the two of us here so that we may be comfortable and happy. Is it possible for us to be happy ultimately through property? Is it possible to be perpetually happy by the possession of material comfort and property? If she becomes the owner of the entire earth, the wealth of the whole world would be hers. In that situation, will she be perpetually happy or will there be some other factor which will intrude upon her happiness in spite of her possession of the values of the entire world?'

Yajnavalkya replied that there was no hope of immortality through wealth and that she would only become one among the many who were well-to-do. When she heard this, Maitreyi asked Yajnavalkya to teach her what he considered as the best. Then Yajnavalkya described to her the greatness of the absolute self, the nature of its existence, the way of attaining infinite knowledge, immortality, etc. This conversation on immortality between Yajnavalkya and Maitreyi is recorded in the *Brihadaranyaka Upanishad.* It is the subject of discourse on the relationship that obtains between eternity and temporality. He said what we call immortality is the life eternal, and that which is temporal is what we see with our eyes. Wealth, in general term, which signifies any kind of value, is any possession. It may be a physical or psychological condition or a social status. Anything that gives comfort, physical or social, can be regarded as a property. This is known as a temporal value. It is temporal as it is in the context of the time process. That which is temporal is conditioned by time.

The happiness, Yajnavalkya said, is the outcome of the transformation that takes place in our mind on account of an imagined connection of the mind with the object that is desired for and possessed. It is a condition of the mind. The mind is a pattern of consciousness. The desire of the mind for a particular object is a desire to get united with that object. Therefore, there is no such satisfaction even after the fulfillment of a desire. No desire, he said, can be fulfilled eternally. That is why, this world is a sorrow, and it shall remain so. There shall be a perpetual effort on the part of the people to grab objects and try to enjoy them. But they cannot enjoy them.

Yajnavalkya told Maitreyi that in reality neither the husband is dear to wife nor the wife is dear to the husband. What is dear is a condition, which they try to bring in their mind by that relation. That condition is always missed and so the expected happiness never comes. Nothing external can give us happiness. Nothing worthwhile exists except *atman* (soul). Finally, everything shall leave us. It is an eternal truth. Everything, he said shall desert us some day or the other. Effect cannot be known unless the cause is known, because the effect is a manifestation of the cause in some proportion.

On the temporal realm of things, Yajnavalkya said that the arrangement is such that things cannot be possessed by any one. The idea of possession is a peculiar notion in the mind. One cannot possess anything except in thought. What we call ownership of property is a condition of mind. There is no vital connection between the thought of the person and the landed property. They only have an imaginary connection. But the social arrangement of the idea of ownership is such that it appears to be well-placed. There is agreement among people that certain ideas should be accepted as logically valid. That is called temporal law. Man-made law is temporal law, and it is valid as long as people who are concerned with it agree.

According to Yajnavalkya, we cannot be happy. We will be very comfortable as are the people who own a lot of wealth, but we should be in the same state in other respects, as is the condition of well-placed people in society. The whole condition of ownership is a condition of the mind, which is an arrangement of psychological values agreed upon by a group of people who have decided that this should be the state of affairs. Nobody can own anything unless it is agreed upon by the concerned people that this idea be accepted. This being the case, how can that bring us permanent satisfaction? The satisfaction of possessing it is conditionally connected with us in a psychological manner, and it cannot be connected unconditionally. What we call permanent happiness is unconditional existence independent of temporal relationship. That unconditional existence is not possible if it is an effect of a conditional arrangement.

Maitreyi asked her husband, then what is the good of all this? Yajnavalkya replied that if one day death is to swallow us and transience is to overwhelm us, impermanence of the world is to threaten us, and if everything is to be insecure at the very start; if all that we regard as worthwhile is, after all, going to be a phantom, as it is not going to assure us as to how long it can be possessed, whether it will be taken away from us and at what time we shall be dispossessed of all the status that we may have in life. If this is the uncertainty of all existence, what good can accrue to us from this that Yajnavalkya is bestowing on her? What then was going to make her perpetually happy, immortal, and satisfied? Then, what is the method she should adopt for the acquisition of the Supreme for final satisfaction?

Maitreyi was keen to know from her husband if she had all the riches in the world, could she still attain immortality. It was surely not possible. All the happiness and conveniences from wealth would not lead us to God. So, Maitreyi then asked why she should acquire wealth if it was not going to deliver her from future rounds of birth and death. She requested her husband to tell her about the Supreme Being for which he was happily giving up household life.

Therefore, Yajnavalkya explained to Maitreyi all about the divine knowledge of the Self. He informed her that no being in this world has any capability of being dear to another without the presence of the soul within. Even to enjoy the beauty of this world one has no meaning without the soul within our own body, for the soul is all that we are. Understanding the depths of spiritual knowledge is the way to attain *moksha*, liberation, from the continued rounds of birth and death. The sage replied that wealth could only make one rich, nothing else. She then asked for the wealth of immortality. Yajnavalkya was happy to hear this and imparted to Maitreyi the doctrine of the soul and his knowledge of attaining immortality. He took *sannyasa* and Maitreyi attained supreme bliss by hearing her husband's discourse and by diving deep into this spiritual understanding. In this way, Maitreyi showed how all women could achieve the heights of spiritual understanding simply by careful listening and practising the Vedic path.

Wisdom of Yajnavalkya is manifest in *Brihadaranyaka Upanishad*, where he gives his teachings to his wife Maitreyi and King Janaka. He also participates in a competition arranged by King Janaka about the selection of great *Brahmajnani*, the knower of Brahman. His intellectual dialogues with Gargi, a learned scholar of the times, form a separate chapter replete with philosophical and mystical question–answers in *Brihadaranyaka Upanishad*. In the end, Yajnavalkya took *Vidvat sannyasa*, renunciation after the attainment of the knowledge of Brahman, and retired to the forest.

Parvati

Parvati, the consort of Shiva and the goddess of love and devotion, is the animating force that brings skill, power, prowess, and genius while she infuses the world with her magic. Fertility, marital felicity, devotion to the spouse, asceticism, and power are different virtues symbolised by Parvati. She is, therefore, worshipped by women to seek her blessings to be an ideal wife. These virtues are highly valued by the Hindu tradition. A literary work, *Saundarya Lahiri*, has described Parvati as the source of all the power in the universe, and Lord Shiva gets all his powers from her. She is considered as a representation of Shakti or *Durga* (inaccessible), the feminine energy of the universe, and is a multi-dimensional goddess. *Shlokas* (hymns) on Parvati form the part of prayers offered to the goddess. Parvati *Shlokas* are as follows:

Sarva Mangala
Maangalye, Shive
Sarvaartha Saadhike
Sharanye Tryambake
Gaurii, Naaraayanii
Namostute

It means—Goddess Parvati is the auspiciousness of all that is auspicious. She is the consort of Lord Shiva, who grants every desire of one's heart. I adore Devi Parvati, who loves all her children. I bow to the Great Mother, who has given refuge to me.'

Maata Cha Paarvati Devi, Pitaa Devo Maheshvara
Baandhavah Shiva Bhaktaacha, Svadesho Bhuvanatrayam

It means—Goddess Parvati is the mother and the divine father is Shiva. The devotees are the children. The world is the creation of these divine beings, and we live on the land of such celestial beings.

The word 'Parvati' is derived from a Sanskrit word, *Parvat*, meaning mountain. In this way, Parvati means one born from mountains and is indicative of the daughter of Himvantha, the personification of Himalayas, or Parvataraja, the king of Oushadhiprastha, and his wife, Menadevi, an *apsara* (fairy). Parvataraja was a devotee of Shiva. He looked after his people justly and virtuously and was also called Giriraja and Shailaraja. His wife was truthful and calm, and was devoted to her husband.

After a while, they had a son who was named Mainaka. Later, Menadevi developed a great desire to have a daughter who should be beautiful and be bestowed with character, knowledge, and wisdom eligible to be Shiva's prospective wife. Menadevi performed her meditation with severe concentration and obtained the favour of Dakshyani (Gowri Devi) who promised that she would be born to her as daughter.

Parvati, in her earlier incarnation, was born in the house of Daksha, one of the progenitors of mankind, and was named as Sati. She was married to Shiva, but she sacrificed her life by self-immolation on a pyre. According to a legend, Daksha instituted a massive sacrifice. Sati, his daughter, attended the ceremony uninvited and against the advice of her husband, Shiva, who was also not invited by his father-in-law. Sati could not bear this insult and entered the sacrificial fire. Hearing the news, Shiva flew into a rage and reacted. Mountains tottered, the earth shook, winds roared, and depth of the sea was disturbed. This catastrophe is described in *Puranas*. Daksha had to acknowledge Shiva's supremacy and apportioned a due share to him.

Menadevi gave birth to a daughter who was named Parvati. The baby did not even suck milk. Everyone was worried as to what should be done. As advised by the family preceptor, sage Gargamuni, Parvataraja had an idol of Shiva brought to the child and got her eyes opened with some treatment. The baby opened her eyes and folded her hands in salutation to the Lord. Butter, which had been offered to Shiva, was put into the child's mouth, and the baby ate it. Thereafter, the baby started sucking milk from the mother's breast. The first sound that the baby pronounced was the name of Lord Shiva. The infant closed her eyes frequently as if she felt the presence of Shiva in her mind.

When she grew up, she showed great interest in playing the game of worshipping Shiva on the sandy banks of the River Ganga. As Parvati was Sati in her previous birth, she still nourished the feelings of devotion to Shiva. Her parents helped her to sustain this devotion. The parents also desired that Parvati should marry Shiva. But Shiva had been deeply hurt by the loss of Sati and had renounced his house in the Kailash Mountains to lead an isolated life. He became an ascetic and resolved not to marry again. Parvataraja went to the place where Shiva was meditating and waited patiently. But, he could not have an access to the exact spot where Shiva was meditating. Eventually, he got the permission for Parvati to come and pray. Parvati attended daily on Shiva, but Shiva's resolve was unshakeable.

At that time, Taraka, a demon, had started tormenting humans and even defeated demi-gods and had taken over the kingdom of heaven. Taraka had a boon from Brahma that only a son of Shiva could kill him. Sati was no more, and Shiva had resolved not to marry. This gave Taraka a feeling of invincibility. In this situation, all demi-gods approached Kama, the demi-god of love, and his consort Rati and assigned to them the task of igniting love for Parvati in Shiva. Kama and Rati went to the place where Shiva was meditating. They waited till he opened his eyes and looked at Parvati. At that moment, Kama let loose his arrow into Shiva's heart. Shiva opened his third eye in the middle of his forehead, and Kama was reduced to ashes. Shiva left. Though Parvati felt hurt, her resolve to marry Shiva became intense. She decided to perform very austere penances to win Shiva's love.

Parvati did extreme *tapasya* (penance), exposing herself to the intense heat of summer and the ice-cold water during the winter. In the beginning, she ate only fruits, but soon she gave up all food and survived only on air. A number of years passed. Shiva came to know of this and was impressed. But with a view to test her, he sent seven sages to dissuade Parvati from wishing to marry him. Sages informed Parvati that Shiva was not a suitable husband for her and that they would find someone else for her. Parvati, however, conveyed her resolve to marry Shiva only. When sages reported Parvati's determination to Shiva, he himself disguised as a youth and went to the place where Parvati was carrying out her penance. He enquired why a young and beautiful woman like herself should subject the self to torture. When Parvati explained her mission, the youth began to laugh and ridicule, stating that the latter was the most unkempt man in the universe and totally incapable of being loved. Parvati didn't want to listen anything against Shiva and asked the youth to leave. When the latter didn't leave, she herself left. She visited Shiva's cave each day to bring him fruit and to sweep the floor of the cave and decorate his cave with flowers. Eventually, she obtained a pledge from Shiva's manservant that he would guard Shiva's bedroom and keep him chaste. A demon disguised itself as Parvati. It seduced Shiva and attempted to kill him by lining its illusory vagina with nails. Shiva was not fooled and put a sword on his penis and vanquished the demon.

Parvati was then told that a woman had visited Shiva. She became furious with the guard who had agreed to protect Shiva. She turned him into a stone. Parvati continued her plans. She lived in the forest and didn't eat anything and had no clothes to protect her tender body from the fierce weather. She invoked Priti and Rati, goddess of love and longing to rouse Shiva out of his meditation. These goddesses entered Shiva's desolate cave and transformed it into a pleasure garden filled with the fragrance of flowers and the buzzing of bees. Guided by Priti and Rati, Kama, the lord of desire, raised his sugarcane bow and shot arrows dripping with desire into the heart of Shiva. Shiva was not amused. He opened his third eye and released the flames of fury that engulfed Kama and reduced his beautiful body to ashes. The death of Kama alarmed the god. They felt that without the lord of desire man will not embrace woman, and he will cease to be. Parvati then thought of another way to conquer Shiva's heart, thinking that when Shiva became her consort, Kama would be reborn. Soon she was able to match Shiva's awesome powers by creating incredible energy in her yoga meditations and gained enough energy to attract the attention of the supreme deity, Brahma.

Brahma took pity on Parvati and asked her what she wanted. Parvati was ashamed of her dark skin and wanted golden skin and Brahma split Parvati into two parts. The horrific black side became Kali while her new skin glowed golden like the Sun. When Shiva saw her and realised how beautiful and powerful Parvati had become, he was unable to resist his temptation to have her as his wife. Her consistent affection soon softened Shiva's heart towards her. The two were married in a sacred ritual performed by gods and spent their honeymoon on the mountains that were the centre of the universe. Parvati kept her promise to the gods. She sent them part of Shiva's aura which, in turn, was given to the river goddess Ganga, who cooled it in her icy waters until it formed a seed.

The seed was planted in the fertile forest floor where it grew into the war God, Skanda. Skanda soon took command, defeated the demons, and restored the Heaven to the gods. But

Parvati longed for a child of her own. Shiva didn't want to father a child. Therefore, he spitefully gave Parvati a scrap of cloth and told her to make a doll and cuddle it instead. She felt hurt by this remark and withdrew to a cave to meditate and get control of her emotions. Grasping the cloth to her breast, Parvati's tears dropped on it, and the cloth grew into the form of Ganesha, her son. She assigned her newly created son to guard over her cave and to keep out all strangers. In the meantime, Shiva began to regret his impulsive act and came to find Parvati and apologise. Ganesha didn't recognise him and blocked his way. Shiva flew into a rage and beheaded Ganesha. Parvati's grief was so intense that Shiva promised to find Ganesha another head. Shiva could only find an elephant's head. Thus, Ganesha was reborn as half human and half elephant. He became the keeper of the threshold, the god of good fortune, and remover of all obstacles to all that is undesirable. His union with Parvati eventually inspired Shiva to accept pleasure into his life, and he soon became the patron of arts. Shiva now became the lord of dance. Shiva revealed the learning that he had gathered in his meditations, ensuring that the energy created by his asceticism was channelled for the good of all mankind.

Shakti, in her milder form, is Parvati, the mountain girl. Uma (the light), Gauri (the yellow-complexioned beauty), Himavati (daughter of Himalaya), Jagatmata (mother of the world), and Bhavani (the goddess of the universe) are her other forms. In her terrible form, she is Durga (inaccessible), Kali or Shyama (the black complexioned), Chandika or Chandi (the fearful one), and Bhairavi (the terrible). All these are broadly included under the name of Devi or Mahadevi, the great goddess.

Once the sage Agastya asked Kartikeya why Parvati, his mother, was called Durga. Kartikeya replied that once upon a time, demon Durga, the son of Ruru, pleased Brahma with his austerities and conquered the three worlds and even dethroned Indra, the king of gods. He abolished all religious ceremonies so that Brahmans were terrified and stopped reading Vedas. Gods assembled and prayed to Shiva to protect them from the tyranny of this demon. Shiva took pity on them and asked Parvati to go and destroy the evil demon. She called the gods and agreed to rescue them from the demon. A long and fierce battle ensued. As soon as the giant came near with his evil followers, Parvati assumed one thousand arms and also brought out a number of weapons out of her body. She repelled every attack, and in the end, the demon assumed the shape of a fearful buffalo, destroying many things. Parvati pierced him with her trident, and the gods praised the goddess and honoured her with the name of Durga.

In the form of Chamundi, Durga, as the name implies, killed two demons, Chanda and Munda. From the forehead of Durga sprang a goddess of jet-black complexion, robed in the hide of an elephant, with a garland of dead corpses. With red-hot eyes and a long tongue, she uttered a big shout and jumped upon the two demons. After this, the Goddess Durga was also named as Chamunda or Chamundi. Goddess Durga has nine important forms, called the Nava-Durga. During the Navaratri festival in October, every year, each of the goddesses is worshipped on a particular night for the destruction of evil and for the preservation of Dharma or righteousness. The nine Durgas are: Shailputri, Brahmacharini as Durga-Shakti, Chandraghanta, Skandamata riding a lion, Katyayan, Kalaratri, Mahagauri, and Siddhidhatri.

Parvati is presented in the Hindu mythology as a beautiful feminine goddess, as a mediator in the conflicts of heaven, as a daughter of the great Himalayas, and as the divine sister of Goddess Ganga. The divine motherly love of Parvati is visible with her two children, Ganapati and Kartikeya. According to Hindu mythology, Parvati is the second consort of Shiva, although she is not different from Dakshyani (Sati), being the reincarnation of that former consort of Lord Shiva. Some people take her as the divine sister of Kali, Lakshmi, Saraswati, Durga, and all other forms of Shakti. She symbolises noble virtues admired by the Hindu religion. The couple, Parvati and Shiva, together symbolises both power of renunciation and asceticism, and the blessings of marital felicity.

Saraswati

In iconography, Goddess Saraswati is shown as wielding in her lotus hands the bell, trident, ploughshare, conch, pestle, discus, bow and arrow, and possessing radiant lustre. She is born from the body of Gowri and is the sustaining base of the three worlds. She is generally shown to have four arms, which represent the four aspects of human personality in learning: mind, intellect, alertness, and ego. These four arms also represent the four Vedas, the primary sacred books for Hindus. The Vedas, in turn, represent the three forms of literature: knowledge, music, and the arts.

In the Vedic system, Saraswati (Sanskrit: सरस्वती *sarasvatī* and Thai: สุรัสวดี Sarasawatee) is the goddess of knowledge, music, and arts. Saraswati has been identified with the Vedic Saraswati River. She is considered as consort of Brahma and wife of Vishnu. Saraswati's children are the three Vedas: *Rigveda* contains hymns representing poetry; *Yajurveda* contains prose; and *Samaveda* represents music. She is also a figure in Mahayana Buddhism, where she first appears in the *Golden Radiance Sutra* of the late fourth or early fifth century.

Saraswati is said to be the daughter of Brahma, the original creative agent, emanating from his mind (*manasa-kanya*). For further creation to continue, Brahma created two beings from his body. One was man and the other was female. The male half was named Swayambhav Manu and the female half was named Shatarupa. Shatarupa is also referred to as Savitri, Gayatri, Saraswati, or Brahmani. Since she had been born from Brahma's body, she was like Brahma's daughter. But Shatarupa was so beautiful that Brahma fell in love with her and wished to marry her. Shatarupa circled Brahma and showed her respects to him. When she stood in front of him, Brahma gazed upon her with the face that he had. But when she went and stood behind him, Brahma could see her no longer. Brahma, obviously, did not want to turn his head. Another head with another face, therefore, sprouted behind Brahma's first head so that he might be able to see Shatarupa. In similar fashion, a head sprouted to Brahma's first head so that he might be able to see Shatarupa. Similarly, a head sprouted to Brahma towards his right and another one to his left. When Shatarupa rose above him, a head sprouted towards the top as well. Thus, Brahma came to have five heads and five faces.

The Rigvedic hymns dedicated to Saraswati mention her as a mighty river with creative, purifying, and nourishing properties. According to Vedas, Maha Saraswati is the presiding 'Goddess of the final episode of Devi Mahatmya'. Here she is believed to be a part of the trinity of Maha Kali, Maha Lakshmi, and Maha Saraswati. She is depicted as eight armed. Her *dhyana shloka* is: *Aim Guru Saraswatyai Namaha*.

Saraswati represents intelligence, consciousness, cosmic knowledge, creativity, education, enlightenment, music, the arts, and power. Hindus worship her not only for 'secular knowledge', but also for 'divine knowledge' essential to achieve *moksha*. She is also referred to as *Shonapunya*, a Sanskrit word meaning 'one purified of blood'. In *Skanda Purana* she is associated with Shiva and in some tantras with Ganesha.

According to Vedanta, she is considered to be the feminine energy and knowledge aspect (shakti) of Brahman, as one of the many aspects of Adi Shakti. As a river/water goddess, Saraswati symbolises fertility and prosperity. She is associated with purity and creativity, especially in the context of communication, such as, in literary and verbal skills. In the post-Vedic age, she began to lose her status as a river goddess and became increasingly associated with literature, arts, music, etc. Her name literally means 'the one who flows', which apparently was applied to thoughts, words, or the flow of a river (in Sanskrit: *dhaara-pravaah*).

The Goddess Saraswati is often depicted as a beautiful, white-skinned woman dressed in pure white often seated on a white *Nelumbo nucifera* lotus, though her actual *vahana* is believed to be a swan, which symbolises that 'she is founded in the experience of the Absolute Truth'. Thus she not only has the knowledge, but also the experience of the highest reality. She is mainly associated with white colour, signifying purity of true knowledge. Occasionally, however, she is also associated with yellow colour, the colour of the flowers of the mustard plant that bloom at the time of her festival in the spring. She is not adorned heavily with jewels and gold, unlike the Goddess Lakshmi, but is dressed modestly—perhaps representing her preference of knowledge over worldly material things.

The four hands also depict this—prose is represented by the book in one hand, poetry by the garland of crystal, and music by the *veena*. The pot of sacred water represents purity in all of these three or their power to purify human thought. She is shown to hold in her hands books, which are the sacred Vedas, representing the universal, divine, eternal, and true knowledge as well as her perfection of the sciences and the scriptures, a *mala* (rosary) of crystals, representing the power of meditation and spirituality, and a pot of sacred water, representing creative and purifying powers. *Veena*, a musical instrument, in her hand represents her perfection of all arts and sciences. Saraswati is also associated with *anuraga*, the love for and rhythm of music, which represents all emotions and feelings expressed in speech or music. It is believed that children born with that name will prove to be very lucky in their studies. Anurag is a great believer in Maha Saraswati.

A 'white swan' or *hansa* in Sanskrit is often located next to her feet. The sacred swan, if offered a mixture of milk and water, is said to be able to drink the milk alone. The swan thus symbolises discrimination between the good and the bad or the eternal and the evanescent. Due to her association with the swan, Goddess Saraswati is also referred to as *Hansa-vahini*, which means—'She who has a swan as her vehicle'. Saraswati is usually depicted near a flowing river, which may be related to her early history as a river goddess. The swan and her association with the lotus flower also point to her ancient origin.

Sometimes a peacock is shown beside the goddess. The peacock represents arrogance and pride over its beauty, and by having a peacock as her mount, the goddess teaches not to be concerned with external appearance and to be wise regarding the eternal truth.

Saraswati *puja* is performed on Basant Panchami, the fifth day of Magha month of Vedic calendar. In several parts of India, generally in southern states, Saraswati pujas are conducted during Navaratri—a nine-day long festival celebrating the power of the feminine aspect of divinity or shakti. Navaratri is celebrated in all goddess temples of India, with great pomp and splendour in south and east India. The last three days of Navaratri, starting from Mahalaya Amavasya (the new moon day) are dedicated to the goddess.

On the ninth day of Navaratri (Mahanavami), books and all musical instruments are ceremoniously kept near the goddess early at dawn and worshipped with special prayers. No studies or any performance of arts are carried out, as it is considered that the goddess herself is blessing the books and the instruments. The festival is concluded on the tenth day of Navaratri (Vijaya Dashami), and the goddess is worshipped again before the books and the musical instruments are removed. It is customary to study on this day, which is called *Vidyarambham*, literally commencement of knowledge. All students are traditionally required to study a part of all that they have learnt till that day, and also to start the study of something new on the same day. Gurus (preceptors) are worshipped on this day as embodiments of Saraswati. In major parts of India, this Navaratri is associated with Goddess Durga, but in southern India Saraswati *puja* is performed. Saraswati's abode is mentioned among the Himalayas in the state of Kashmir. Her favourite fruit is supposed to be the apple. Invocation to Saraswati is embodied in Saraswati vandana mantra, which reads as follows:

Yaa Kundendu Tushaara Haaradhavalaa, Yaa shubhravastraavritha

Yaa Veenavara Dandamanditakara, Yaa Shwetha Padmaasana

Yaa Brahmaachyutha Shankara Prabhutibhir Devaisadaa Vanditha

Saa Maam Paatu Saraswatee Bhagavatee Nihshesha Jaadyaapahaa

When rendered in English it means—'May Goddess Saraswati who is fair like the jasmine-coloured moon; whose pure white garland is like frosty dew drops; who is adorned in radiant white attire; on whose beautiful arm rests the veena and whose throne is a white lotus; who is surrounded and respected by the gods, protect me. May you fully remove my lethargy, sluggishness, and ignorance.'

Saraswati is again described as the wife or the Shakti of Brahma, and as such, she has, like Brahma, the swan as her carrier. Somewhere she is described as emanating from the mouth of Lord Krishna, somewhere as the daughter of Shiva by Durga. In the worship of Mother Durga, in autumn, Lakshmi and Saraswati accompany the mother as the two daughters, or the three may represent the Shaktis of Shiva, Vishnu, and Brahma.

Saraswati finds a place as an important goddess in Buddhism as well as in Jainism with iconographical details. In later Buddhism, however, she is generally associated with Manjushri, the god of all learning. In the Buddhist liturgical texts, she is variously described as Maha Saraswati, Aryavajra-Saraswati, Vajravina-Saraswati, Vajra-Saradha, etc. She presents a variety of names and iconographical differences in Jainism as well.

According to *Brahma Vaivarta Purana*, she is associated with Shiva and in some tantras with Ganesha. According to *Brahma Vaivarta Purana*, Vishnu has three wives, who constantly quarrel with each other so that eventually he keeps only Lakshmi, giving Ganga to Shiva, and Saraswati to Brahma. In the *Rigveda*, Saraswati is credited in association with Indra, with killing of Vritraasura, a demon who hoarded the entire earth's water, and therefore, represents drought, darkness, and chaos. She is often seen as equivalent to other Vedic goddesses such as Vak, Savitri, and Gayatri. She is not only worshipped for secular knowledge, but also for the true divine knowledge essential to achieve *moksha*. She is also referred to as *Shonapunya*, a Sanskrit word meaning 'one purified of blood'.

Saraswati has four hands representing four aspects of human personality in learning: mind, intellect, alertness, and ego. She has sacred scriptures in one hand and a lotus—the symbol of true knowledge—in the second. With her other two hands, she plays the music of love and life on a string instrument called the *veena*. Her four arms also represent the four Vedas—the primary sacred books for Hindus. The Vedas, in turn, represent the three forms of literature—*Rigveda* contains hymns representing poetry, *Yajurveda* contains prose, *Samaveda* represents music.

The hymns in praise of the River Saraswati in the *Rigveda* and the homage paid to her often make one believe that Saraswati was not always regarded as a mere river; there was a latent belief in a presiding deity over the river. In one verse of the *Rigveda*, Saraswati has been praised as the best among the mothers, best among the rivers, and best also among the goddesses, and as such, she had a share in the oblations offered in the sacrifices. In the next phase of her evolution, we find her identified with *vach* or word. And that became the turning point in her evolution as the goddess of learning not only in India, but also in some other neighbouring or eastern countries like Tibet, Java, and Japan, where stone images of the goddess have been discovered. In the Vedic literature, Goddess Saraswati is often associated with two other goddesses, Ida and Bharati. Some people have interpreted the three goddesses as three aspects of the same goddess of speech. It is said that at one time, both the Gandharavas (celestial minstrels) and the gods tried to win over the Vag Devi by pleasing and propitiating her by songs and by playing on the lyre. These legends give us a clue how Saraswati began to evolve as the goddess of learning and of all fine arts in later times.

Sati

In Hinduism, Daksha, 'the skilled one', is an ancient creator god, one of the Prajapatis (creator deity), the Rishi and the Adityas, and a son of Aditi and Brahma. Yet, in Kashyapa, another source, he is said to be the father of Diti and Aditi, Kashyapa's wives and Sati's sisters. With his wife Prasuti, Daksha is the father of thirteen daughters. One of his daughters (often said to be the youngest) was Shakti who had always wished to marry Shiva. Daksha forbade it, but she disobeyed him and did so anyway, finding in Shiva a doting and loving husband. Daksha disliked Shiva intensely, calling him a dirty, roaming ascetic, and reviling the great yogi's cohort of goblins and ghouls.

Yet, according to another story in almost all *Puranas*, Prajapati Daksha's eldest daughter Sati was married to Shiva after she developed love for him much against the wishes of her father, Daksha. Daksha distanced himself from his daughter, and his son-in-law, Shiva. Once, Daksha Prajapati had organised a grand *Ashwamedha Yajna* (horse sacrifice) to which he had invited all his daughters and son-in-laws except Sati and Rudra. He consciously excluded Sati from the list of invitees. He also set up a statue of Shiva at the entrance of his hall, which he defiled and mocked. Sati, ebullient at the thought of such a great event, and assuming that the daughter of the king was welcome no matter what, attended the festival. Snubbed by her father and treated with disdain, Sati nonetheless maintained her composure. Sati, eventually, reached her father's place much against the advice of Shiva, who was strictly against going to a place uninvited.

Shiva's apprehensions were not unfounded, as Sati was indeed humiliated by Daksha in front of all the esteemed guests. At this, Sati asked her father, 'Who except you can be hostile to Shiva, who is free from enmity and is the soul of all, whom none can excel in this world, and who being the dear self of embodied beings, knows no favourite or otherwise? The most generous men feel inclined to magnify the smallest virtues, but you discovered vice in these. It is no wonder that great men always censure with intolerance those wicked people who hold that the body (itself) is the soul . . . Alas, you, an unlucky person, hate that Shiva of holy fame and inviolable command whose disyllabic name (Shiva), pronounced for even a single time in the course of conversation, immediately destroys one's sin. You revolt against that friend of all whose lotus feet shower blessings on the supplicating world. Did Brahma and the gods, other than yourself, who hold on their crests (flowers) touched by his feet, not know that God named Shiva as an inauspicious being who lived with goblins on the cremation ground, spreading out his matted hair and wearing the garlands, ashes, and skulls of that place? If incapable (of redress), one should leave the place by closing one's ears when the Lord (Shiva), the protector of religion (dharma) is freely decried by men; but if capable, one should tear out by force the denouncing tongues of the wicked and then give up one's own life, that is dharma. So, I shall no longer sustain this body produced from you who censure that dark-throated (god) because as people say, the vomiting out of the condemned food eaten through mistake leads to purification.'

Sati told her father that she was ashamed to be his daughter and would not like to be called Daksha's daughter. She, therefore, expressed her resolve to give up her physical body that her father had owed to her by immolating herself. She even cursed her father to be born on earth as the son of the ten Prachetas, when he would try to perform an *Ashwamedha Yajna* (horse sacrifice).

Daksha tried to pacify Sati, telling her that she is the mother of the universe, and if she died, how the universe would survive. To this, Sati replied that she was unable to negate what she had said. However, she granted him the boon that when he is born on this earth, he will continue his devotion to her. Sati told her father that, henceforth, she would be known by one hundred and eight names and she would be known by these names in eight *tirthas* (holy places). Some of these names are: Vishalakshi at Varanasi, Lingadharini at Naimisha, Lalitadevi at Prayaga, Kamakshi at Gandhamadana, Kumuda at Manasa, Vishvakaya at Ambara, Gomati at Gomanta, Kamacharini at Mandara, Madotkata at Chaitraratha, Jayanti at Hastinapura, Gouri at Kanyakuvja, Rambha at Malayachala, Kirtimati at Ekamra, and Vishva at Vishveshvara.

Sati was so deeply hurt by her father's rude behaviour and the manner in which he made fun of her husband that having recited these names, Sati then took her seat on the ground, closed her eyes, and reduced her body to ashes by the yogic fire produced internally by abstract meditation on Shiva. When Rudra learnt about Sati's death, he cursed Daksha by saying that he would lose his divine status and would be born as a human being in the lineage of Dhruva. In her next birth, Sati was born as the daughter of Himalaya and Menakadevu. She was once again successful in getting Shiva as her husband by virtue of her deep devotion towards Shiva.

According to another version, when on the occasion of *Ashwamedha Yajna*, Sati came to know of the shameless insults to her husband in his absence, and the repeated slights King Daksha and his courtiers railed at Shiva, she committed suicide in grief for her beloved. Hearing the news, Shiva's attendants rushed inside the ceremony hall and started attacking all the guests present there. However, the demons invoked by Bhrigu defeated Shiva's attendants, and they retreated back to his abode. Upon hearing the news of his beloved wife's death, Shiva was infuriated that Daksha could so callously cause the harm of his (Daksha's) own daughter in so ignoble manner. Shiva grabbed a lock of his matted hair and dashed it to the ground. From the two pieces rose the ferocious Virabhadra and the terrible Rudrakali, while Bhadrakali arose from the wrath of the *devi* herself. Upon Shiva's orders, they stormed the ceremony and killed Daksha as well as many of the guests. Terrified with remorse others propitiated Lord Shiva and begged his mercy to restore Daksha's life and to allow the sacrifice to be completed. Shiva, who is merciful, restored Daksha's life with the head of a goat. In his humility, and repentance for his graceless and sinful acts, Daksha became one of Shiva's most devoted attendants.

After the death of Shiva's first love—Sati, Shiva isolated himself into a dark cave buried amongst the snow covered peaks of the Himalayas. He rejected the world outside, as he was distraught by the loss of his first true love. Meanwhile, the demons, lead by Taraka, rose from the netherworld and drove the *devas*, gods, out of the heavens. The gods sought a warrior who would help them regain the celestial realm. Brahma then informed that only Shiva could father such a warrior. But Shiva was immersed in meditation and was oblivious to the problems of the gods. The gods invoked the mother goddess, who appeared before them as Kundalini, a coiled serpent. This Shakti proclaimed that she would coil herself around Shiva, wean out his knowledge and energy for the good of the world and make Shiva father a child. Thereupon, Shakti took birth as Parvati, daughter of the Himavan, lord of the mountains, determined to draw Shiva out of his cave and make him her consort.

Sati incarnated as Parvati in her next life, and remarried Shiva, henceforth, never to part with him again. It is for this reason that Shiva, while monogamous, has had two wives in reality, but the same soul in two incarnations.

Parvati was like *bogashakti*, *boga*, pleasure, *shakti*, goddess, energy, priti and rati. Everyday, Parvati would visit Shiva's cave, sweep the floor, decorate it with flowers, and offer him fruits, hoping to win his love. But Shiva never opened his eyes to look upon her charming face. Exasperated, the goddess invoked Priti and Rati, goddess of love and longing to rouse Shiva out of his meditation. These goddesses entered Shiva's desolate cave and transformed it into a pleasure garden filled with the fragrance of flowers and the buzzing of bees. Guided by Priti and Rati, Kama, the lord of desire, raised his sugarcane bow and shot arrows dripping with desire into the heart of Shiva. Shiva was not amused. He opened his third eye and released the flames of fury that engulfed Kama and reduced his beautiful body to ashes. The death of Kama alarmed the gods. They felt that without the lord of desire man will not embrace woman and he will cease to be. Parvati then thought of another way to conquer Shiva's heart, thinking that when Shiva becomes her consort, Kama would be reborn.

Parvati went into the forest and performed rigorous *tapas* (austerities), wearing nothing to protect her tender body from the harsh weather, eating nothing, not even a leaf, and earning the admiration of forest ascetics who named her Aparna. Aparna matched Shiva in her capacity to cut herself from the world and completely master her physical needs. The power of her *tapas* shook Shiva out of his meditation. He stepped out of his cave and accepted Parvati as his wife. Shiva married Parvati in the presence of the gods following the sacred rites and took her to the highest peak of the cosmos, Mount Kailasa, the pivot of the universe. As the world revolved around them, the two became one, and Kama was reborn.

Parvati melted Shiva's stern heart with her affection. Together they played dice on Mount Kailas or sported on the banks of Lake Manasarovar, discovering the joys of married life. Thus, the goddess awakened Shiva's concern for the world by questioning him on various issues. As he spoke, he revealed the secrets of the Tantras and the Vedas that he had gathered while in meditation. Inspired by her beauty, Shiva became the fountainhead of the arts of dance and drama. He sang and danced to the delight of the gods who were pleased to see his enchantment with the goddess.

Parvati gave Shiva's aura to the gods. She said that from this would rise the warlord. The gods gave Shiva's aura to Svaha, consort of Agni, the fire god. Unable to bear the heat of the aura and the God Agni for long, Svaha gave the aura to Ganga, the river goddess who cooled it in her icy waters and Shiva's aura turned into a seed. Aranyani, the goddess of the forest, embedded the divine seed in the fertile forest floor where it was transformed into a robust child with six heads and twelve arms. Six forest nymphs called the Krittkas found this magnificent child in a lotus. Overcome by maternal affection they began nursing him. The six-headed son of Shiva, born of many mothers, came to be known as Kartikeya. Parvati taught Kartikeya the art of war and turned him into the celestial warlord called Skanda. Skanda took command of the celestial armies, defeated Taraka in battle, and restored the heavens to the gods. This guardian of the heavens went on to destroy many demons who opposed the reign of the gods. But, he could not defeat the demon Raktabija. Whenever this demon's blood touched the ground, a thousand new demons sprang to life. He seemed unconquerable.

To aid her son in his endeavour to rid the three worlds of the demons, Parvati entered the cosmic battlefield as the dreaded Goddess Kali, dark as death and with dishevelled hair covering her naked body. Kali spread her tongue over the battlefield and licked the demon's falling blood, catching on her long, outstretched tongue before the drop could find its way to the ground, springing a new demonic life. Raktabija, without his multiplying numbers, was left powerless. Skanda was able to dispatch Raktabija and all his remaining duplicates with ease. Skanda thanked his mother for her timely help. To celebrate her victory, Kali danced wildly on the battlefield, bedecking herself with a garland of served heads and a girdle of severed hands. Intoxicated with Raktabija's blood, Kali ran amuck across the three worlds, destroying everything and everyone in her sight. To restrain her, Shiva took the form of a corpse and blocked her path. As the goddess, blinded by bloodlust, tripped on his lifeless body, she was jolted out of her frenzy. She wondered if she had killed her own husband. She placed a foot on Shiva's chest and brought him back to life.

Shiva then took the form of a little child and began to cry, stirring maternal love in the heart of Kali. This forced her to shed her fierce form. Kali became Gauri, the radiant mother, bestower of life. Gauri told Shiva that she wanted a child. But Shiva was not interested in a family. He turned away from her and went into the forest to perform *tapas*. Determined to be a mother, Parvati/Gauri decided to create a son for herself without the aid of her husband. She scrubbed her skin with sandal paste, scrapped off the dead skin, mixed it with clay and moulded out of it a beautiful doll into which she breathed life. She ordered her newly created son to keep watch over her cave and keep out all strangers. When Shiva returned from Kailas, Parvati's son failed to recognise his mother's consort and prevented him from entering the cave. Initiated by the child's insolence, Shiva raised his trident and cut off his head. When Parvati saw her son's headless body, she wept and out of her tears came her fierce handmaidens, the Yoginis, who threatened to destroy the whole world. To placate Parvati, Shiva resurrected the child by placing an elephant's head on the severed neck. Shiva also accepted Ganesh, Parvati's created son, as the first of his sons. Ganesh, who had prevented Shiva from crossing the threshold of his mother's cave, became keeper of thresholds, an obstacle to all that is undesirable. He who seeks access to the wisdom, bounty, and mystery of nature worships Ganesh, the beloved son and sacred doorkeeper of Shakti.

With Parvati by his side, Shiva became a family man. But he did not abandon his ways as a hermit. He continued to meditate and immersed himself in narcotic dreams. His carefree attitude, and his refusal to shoulder household responsibilities sometimes angered Parvati. But then she would come to terms with his unconventional ways and make peace. The consequent marital bliss between Shakti and Shiva ensured harmony between matter and spirit and brought stability and peace to the cosmos. Parvati thus became Ambika, goddess of the household of marriage, motherhood, and family.

Amongst the goddesses known as the *matris*, Sati is known by the name, Vaishnavi. A sati is a woman who is devoted to her husband. Amongst all such satis, the goddess is known as Arundhati. She is known as Tilottama amongst all women, as Brahmakala in mind, and as Shakti in the body.

Savitri

Savitri and Satyavan lived the life of an ideal couple whose story, as narrated by Markandeya, appears in *The Book of the Forest* of the *Mahabharata*. When Yudhisthira, the eldest Pandu brother, asked Markandeya whether there had ever been a woman whose devotion matched that of Draupadi, Markandeya replied by relating this story.

Ashwapati, king of Madra, didn't have any child. The king was keen to have a son for his lineage. He performed thousands and thousands of *yajnas* (sacrifices) and offered oblations to Sun God Savitr. The Sun God was pleased with the king's devotion and prayers. Eventually, the Sun God Savitr appeared before the king and said, 'You will not have a son. But I am going to grant you a heroic daughter.' The king felt happy at the prospect of a child. In due course, the child was born. The daughter was named Malati. But since she was born as a result of a boon received from the Sun God Savitr, she was more popularly known as Savitri. Since Savitri was born out of devotion and asceticism, she practised the necessary traits.

Savitri was quite beautiful and pure. Princess Savitri was brought up amidst luxuries. She was given a liberal education. As the years passed, she blossomed into a beautiful, intelligent, and gentle girl. She was imbued with great courage and was adept in the performance of her varied duties. As a result of this, her own people and that of the adjacent countries held her in great respect. But she was so calm and dignified that the young princes of her time could not think of wooing her as a wife. Thus, she remained unmarried.

One day, the princess after her bath offered oblations at the altar, and going to her father, who sat on his throne, reverently worshipped him with flowers. The king blessed his accomplished daughter and said, 'My daughter, the time is ripe for giving you in marriage. Yet none has come asking me for your hand. Therefore, you choose a husband worthy of you and let me know. I shall consider and bestow you on the man on whom your choice falls.' With blushing cheeks, Savitri bowed and left the royal presence.

The king made preparations for her to go out on a long excursion to select for herself a prospective husband. She was escorted by her father's old counsellors as well as attendants. She left the palace in a golden chariot. But instead of going to the palaces of other kings, she went to the woods and visited the hermitages of the royal sages. Days and months passed in this way, but she could not meet her prospective husband. After travelling for a long distance, she saw a young man carrying an axe on his shoulder and a bundle of wood in his arm. The charming personality of this unknown young man captured her attention, and she felt that it was he with whom she was destined to spend her life. After making proper enquiries, she returned home to tell her parents of her choice.

On reaching the royal court, Savitri saw sage Narada, the celestial sage, along with the king's ministers. Savitri told her father that there was a noble king named Dyumatsena ruling over the Shalwa country. He had only one son. As ill luck would have it, the king became blind and his enemies, taking advantage of this, attacked his kingdom and drove him out. The king accompanied by his wife and infant son left for the forest. There he tried to forget the world, which had treated him so cruelly by practising austerities and meditations. The prince was brought up in the hermitage, where he had grown up and still lived with his venerable parents. Savitri told her father that she chose the youth named Satyavat (Satyavan) as her lord. Sage Narada immediately warned the king not to marry his daughter with Satyavat, as Satyavat 'is bright as the sun, wise as Brihaspati, the preceptor of the gods, brave as Indra, the lord of the gods, and forgiving as the earth', but was not suitable for Savitri as he was destined to live only for one year.

Savitri shuddered for a moment and trembled. The king asked his daughter to choose another person as her lord. Savitri thought for a moment and immediately gained confidence, shedding her shyness. She felt awakened to her full sense of dignity. She replied, 'To die can fall but once. A daughter can be given away but once. And once only can a person say, "I give away." Indeed, whether he has a short or a long life, whether he possesses virtues or is devoid of them, I have selected my husband for once, and I will not select a second man.'

The king had to bow to the will of his daughter. Sage Narada felt overwhelmed by the devotion, chastity, and determination of Savitri and gave her his blessings. On the auspicious day, the royal couple took their daughter to the hermitage of Dyumatsena, where the marriage was solemnised. The king gave the newly married couple costly presents. Savitri was quite happy.

But as soon as her parents left, she put away all her costly things, and dressed herself like the daughter-in-law of a hermit. She attended to the needs of her old mother-in-law and tenderly served her blind father-in-law. Her deep love for the family members and solicitude for them won the heart of her husband. Yet the words of Narada invariably echoed in her mind.

A good deal of time elapsed. The day came when only four days were left for the day when, according to Narada, her husband was to expire. Three days before the foreseen death of Satyavan, Savitri took a vow of fasting and vigil. Her father-in-law told her that she had taken on too harsh of a regime, but Savitri replied that she took an oath to perform these austerities, at which Dyumatsena offered his support. She took up the very difficult vow of *Triratra* (three nights' penance). The old king affectionately asked Savitri to forego the vow. But Savitri was firm in her resolve and said, 'Don't worry, dear father, I have taken up this vow, and with your blessings I shall be able to keep it.' In this process, she became frail and pale. Everybody around her felt the presence of a divine spirit in her. Eventually, it was now the designated day. Throughout the last night, Savitri kept her lone vigil. Her eyes were tearless and her prayers now became intense. As and when the appointed hour drew near, she was afraid of losing her dear husband, but she never disclosed her fears to her husband or anybody else in the family. When she was asked to take her food, she said that she would break her fast when the sun would set.

In the morning of Satyavan's predicted death, Savitri asked for her father-in-law's permission to accompany her husband into the forest. Since she had never asked for anything during the entire year she had spent at the hermitage, Dyumatsena granted her wish.

When she saw her husband, Satyavat, ready to leave for forest she decided to accompany him. The couple reached the middle of the forest. Satyavat asked Savitri to sit under a tree. He collected some sweet and juicy fruits for her and started cutting the branches of trees with his axe. While Satyavan had been splitting wood, he suddenly became weak and laid his head on Savitri's lap. She had been carefully looking at her husband moving the axe fast, which gradually became slow and then it stopped. She had also seen her husband coming towards her with dragging feet and sweat on his brows. He now complained of terrible headache and weakness. Savitri trembled with fear and took her husband under the shade of a tree. She made him lie on the ground with his head on her lap. She realised that it was the fateful moment.

All of a sudden, Savitri saw a dark, crowned figure with red eyes, clad in red, and carrying a noose, standing before her and looking at Satyavat. She gently placed her husband's head on the ground, rose and with a beating heart respectfully asked the visitor who he was. He was Yama, the god of death. Yama tied up Satyavan's minute body in a noose and prepared to take it to his abode. But when Yama left, Savitri followed him. 'Where do you think you are going?' asked Yama. 'There is no greater duty for a wife than serving her husband. Since my husband is leaving, I have to accompany him.' Yama said, 'I am pleased at your devotion—Ask for a boon, and I shall grant it to you. The only thing that you cannot ask for is that Satyavan be brought back to life.'

'My father-in-law has become blind', replied Savitri. 'He can, therefore, no longer be the king. Please grant me the boon that his eyesight be restored so that he could become the king again.' 'I grant you that,' said Yama. 'Now, please return. You will unnecessarily get tired if you follow me.'

'How can I get tired if I follow you?' asked Savitri. 'You are the chief of all the gods. Is it possible to get tired if one follows you?'

'That pleases me even more,' said Yama. 'Ask for another boon. But under no circumstances are you allowed to ask that Satyavat be brought back to life.' 'My father has no sons,' replied Savitri. 'Please grant me the boon that he may have a hundred sons.' 'I grant you that,' said Yama and continued, 'Now return. Go and perform your husband's funeral rites. Serve your parents and parents-in-law well. You are unnecessarily tiring yourself by following me around.'

'I thank you for your advice', replied Savitri. 'But I have already told you that I cannot possibly get tired. You are the lord of dharma and righteousness. Can one possibly tire oneself by following such a person?'

'Your devotion is truly amazing. Ask for another boon. But do not ask for Satyavan's life.' At this, Savitri asked for a boon that she and Satyavan be blessed with one hundred sons. Yama granted the boon without thinking. Savitri then pointed out that what Yama had agreed to would be impossible if Satyavan died. Yama had no option but to restore Satyavan to life. Yama blessed Savitri and went away.

Satyavan awakened as though he had been in a deep sleep and returned to his parents along with his wife. Meanwhile, at their home, Dyumatsena regained his eyesight before Savitri and Satyavan returned. Since Satyavan still did not know what had happened, Savitri related the story to her parents-in-law, husband, and the gathered ascetics. As they praised her, Dyumatsena's ministers arrived with news of the death of his usurper. The king and his entourage returned to his kingdom with great joy.

In due course, Satyavan and Savitri had one hundred sons. Thus, over the years, Savitri became a model for all devoted wives to follow. To commemorate and to emulate the attributes of Savitri, Hindu wives observe fast for the welfare and longevity of their husbands.

The name of Savitri in the epic *Mahabharata* has become immortal as an ideal wife. Her memory is cherished not only in every Hindu home, but also by those outside the fold. She set an example before the married women in India to do everything possible to sustain their relationship with their consorts and pray for their longevity. Orthodox Hindu wives still observe fast for three days in the month of *Jyaishtha* (May–June) in her honour.

Shakuntala

The epic *Mahabharata* tells the story of the noble descendants of King Bharat from whose name India, i.e., Bharat originated. Bharat was the son of Shakuntala and Dushyanta. This story is also the subject matter of Kalidasa's famous play in Sanskrit, *Abhijnanasakuntala*.

Shakuntala in both the epic and Kalidasa's play is shown as the daughter of the royal sage Vishwamitra and Menaka, the celestial nymph. Long ago, the powerful sage Vishwamitra is shown in the play as engaged in concentrated meditation, great austerities, and penance that would give him almost absolute power over kingdom of earth and heaven. The king of Heaven, Indra, is shaken to know this effort of Vishwamitra that could pose danger to his throne. Therefore, Indra decides to put obstacles in his austerities and thereby break his *sadhana*, spiritual discipline.

Indra thinks of using the weapon of lust and deputes the most beautiful and ever youthful *apsara*, Menaka, from heaven to distract and seduce Vishwamitra. She descends down to earth from heaven and tries to tempt Vishwamitra by various charming dances and songs. After some efforts, Vishwamitra is lured by the beauty and youthful attraction. They are married, and the *tapas* (austerities) of Vishwamitra are broken. A beautiful daughter is born to them who is later named Shakuntala.

But Menaka has to return to heaven. Therefore, they leave the child amidst a beautiful garden near a lake. A swan in the lake sees the crying child and gives it some water. Just then a sage named Kanva, who is passing by, sees the swan giving water to the child. In this way, the child is being protected by birds (*Shakunton* in Sanskrit), and, therefore, she is named Shakuntala. The sage Kanva decides to take the child home and names it 'Shakuntala', which means one fed by a swan. Vishwamitra, whose *tapas* are broken, leaves for forest to retreat. Rishi Kanva brings up the child. Shakuntala blossoms as a most beautiful lady under the loving care of Rishi Kanva.

One day, King Dushyanta, while on a hunting expedition, pursues a male deer wounded by his arrow. He leaves his attendants and all emblems of royalty and walks into the holy retreat. He reaches sage Kanva's ashram. In the words of Kalidasa, in *Abhijnanasakuntalam,* Shakuntala and her two companions were watering the plants at that time with sisterly affection and

Shakuntala was nursing the wounded deer when the king ushers in. He first chooses to eavesdrop on all the young women and then introduces himself as an officer of the king. Of the three girls, Shakuntala captures his fancy. Shakuntala appears to him as beautiful as the goddess of fortune, but dressed as an ascetic. In the course of his lively conversation with her, he observes her closely in her changing moods. Every fleeting moment brings a new view of her perfect form. He then feels that Shakuntala is his suitable bride. The king feels sorry and profusely begs Shakuntala for harming the deer.

Shakuntala comes out of the hermitage and invites the king to enter the cottage. The king, after introducing himself, tells her that he has come to pay his respects to the great sage Kanva. The young lady told the king that her father has gone to gather fruits and would return soon.

Shankuntala's first upsurge of love is described by the poet Kalidasa as a departure from the sacred ethos of the hermitage. She is so shaken by her friends that she loses hope of her normal recovery. The friends guess that she could be the victim of Cupid's 'arrows'. They can judge Shakuntala's love for Dushyanta. Therefore, they arrange a secret union of the lovers without consulting any of the elders. Further two cantos of Kalidasa's play depict the stages of love between the two.

Dushyanta and Shakuntala fall in love with each other. The king proposes to Shakuntala. They are married according to the Gandharva* rites, while still basking in the initial euphoria of

---

*Gandharva marriage (marriage of the celestials) involves simple exchange of garlands. We find references of this type of wedding in Hindu mythologies and epics. This is equivalent to eloping in today's world, and couples whose union is not blessed by families seek refuge in this custom. It is a form of love marriage.

love. As an evidence of his office, the king shows her the ring with his own name Dushyanta inscribed on it. Dushyanta gets ready to leave for his capital and promises to have a huge escort sent to her later to bring her to the capital. But before leaving, he gives his precious ring to Shakuntala, cautioning her not to lose it. After the king's departure, everything goes downhill for Shakuntala. The king never sends his retinue.

Shakuntala becomes pregnant. One day, a powerful rishi, Durvasa, comes to the ashram. Since Shakuntala is lost in her thoughts about Dushyanta, she fails to greet him properly. Incensed by this slight, the rishi curses Shakuntala, saying that the person she is dreaming of would forget about her altogether. As Durvasa is about to depart in a rage, one of Shakuntala's friends quickly explains to him the reason for Shakuntala's distraction. The rishi, realising that his extreme wrath is not warranted, modifies his curse, saying that the person who has forgotten Shakuntala would remember everything again if she shows him a personal token that had been given to her.

After some days, Shakuntala wonders why Dushyanta has not returned to her. Her worry almost turned into panic because of the fact that she is pregnant. Soon, her condition reveals the truth. Rishi Kanva and ladies of the ashram notice the change in Shakuntala. On enquiring, the truth becomes known to all. Rishi Kanva had brought up Shakuntala as her own daughter, and hence, he decides to send her to her husband, King Dushyanta, where she should be accepted as Dushyanta's queen. On the way, they cross a river by a canoe ferry. Shakuntala feels charmed by the deep blue waters of the river and runs her fingers through the water. Her ring slips off her finger, and she doesn't realise it.

Shakuntala reaches the court of Dushyanta. A message is sent to the king of the arrival of a woman who claims to be his wife. Dushyanta, under the influence of the ascetic's curse, disowns Shakuntala in open court, dashing her hopes, and crushing her reputation. He had lost his memory about Shakuntala and all about their stay together. But there, in the midst of tremendous obstructive circumstances, Shakuntala shows her nobility, chastity, dignity, and trustfulness and makes a spirited defence of herself and her position. The king, however, refuses to accept Shakuntala as his wife.

Shakuntala, as the daughter of a nymph and the daughter of a great ascetic, turns her humiliation into an angry woman. But all her words are of no avail. She tries to remind her husband about the night they had spent together in the forest ashram of Rishi Kanva, etc., but still of no avail. The king had forgotten that part of his life. Shakuntala tells him about the ring and tries to show it to him, but she is not able to find it on her finger. Shakuntala is now like Sita in the epic *Ramayana*, calling the earth-goddess to split and take her in when she has failed to remind Dushyanta of his promise to marry him.

Frustrated at this, Shakuntala leaves for the forest all alone and decides to give birth to the child. Gradually, her self-confidence returns and her fear vanished. She lives in the penance grove of Maricha and learns the lessons of suffering. In due course, she gives birth to a most beautiful and intelligent son. The boy is named Bharat. Bharat blossoms into a strong youth. His only human companion now is his mother. He starts playing with wild animals and rides on them as one rides horses. The mother teaches him as a prince. He opens the mouths of tigers and lions to count their teeth.

Meanwhile, a fisherman is surprised to find a royal ring in the belly of a fish he has caught. He recognises the royal seal and takes the ring to the palace. Upon seeing his ring, Dushyanta's memories of Shakuntala flashes into his mind. An old curse of forgetfulness laid on the king is broken and the king is repentant and becomes subdued. He immediately sets out to find her. He reaches her father's ashram, but she is no longer there. He goes deeper into the forest to find out Shakuntala. There he finds a young boy opening the mouth of a lion. The boy is counting its teeth. The king greets the boy. He is amazed by the boy's boldness and strength and asks his name. He feels surprised when the boy answers that he is Bharat, the son of King Dushyanta. The boy takes him to Shakuntala. Shakuntala and her son are accepted with dignity and reverence by Dushyanta. The child—the utmost limit of affection, the most powerful link to bind parents to each other, the finest efflorescence in Kalidasa's creed of love—is introduced, thus reuniting the family.

Amazed at the whole spectacle, the king, in the words of Kalidasa in his play thus speaks

> In a dusty apparel, grey appearing
> With a face penance, impaired; with hair unknotted;
> So unkind as I was, yet chaste her bearing
> From myself, parted so long, remains devoted.

The king realises and admits his folly of unbridled passion.

Thus, Shakuntala, the fine character in the *Mahabharata* and Kalidasa's *Abhijnanasakuntalam* has been the finest and the most striking specimen of romantic love. Although born of a heavenly nymph, she is shown essentially as human. She errs, suffers, corrects herself, and is elevated and transported into the galaxy of great women. She has in her very blood the ingredients of passion inherited from her mother. Environment in her case came in direct conflict with heredity. Her curt comments, primitive as well as sophisticated turns of expression, her prolonged sidelong glances, her love-malady, her sensuous love epistle, her self-denunciation at her own coyness at first meetings—all these prepare us for the catastrophe that overtakes her. Absent-mindedness on the king's departure deflects her from the duty of giving due reception to a guest, and this is visited by severe punishment. Rishi Durvasa inflicts on her a curse that is inevitable, but nonetheless painful.

Above all, the character of Shakuntala as illustrated in the great epic and in Kalidasa's *Abhijnanasakuntala*, holds a mirror to the sufferings in human life as rooted in the human psyche. If the lovers have to suffer untold agony, it is because of their own failings, rooted in their character. The heroine is a fondly brought up daughter in sage Kanva's hermitage. The character brings up a clear-cut conflict between the ethos of the ascetic hermitage and the deceptive behaviour of the hero-king. Fate brings King Dushyanta to this hermitage on a pretext of hunting. Quite symbolically, the background suggests that the king's party was hunting down harmless deer in the hermitage without any compunction. This is a premonition of what is in store for the deer-like girl who is destined to meet the king and is caught in the web as an unsuspecting victim.

The much delayed happy ending involves not merely the union of parted lovers, but a triumph of conjugal felicity completed with the acquisition of a child, thus establishing the fact that essence of the joy of life lies in pure, sacred, and ever-widening love.

Sita

Sita, also spelled as Seeta, is a legendary figure in Hindu mythology whose life and activities have been described in Valmiki's *Ramayana* as well as Tulsidas's *Ramcharitramanas*. She is known by many names. As the daughter of King Janaka, she is referred to as Janaki; as the princess of Mithila, she is Mythili or Maithili; and as the wife of Rama, she is called Ramaa. Her father, Janaka, earned the sobriquet 'Videha' due to his ability to transcend body consciousness. Sita, therefore, is also known as Vaidehi (Vaidehi or Vaydehi). Above all, she is best known by the name 'Sita', which literally means 'furrow'. The word 'furrow' was a poetic term in ancient India, its imagery redolent of fecundity and the many blessings accrued from settled agriculture. The Sita of the *Ramayana* may have been named after a more ancient Vedic goddess. Sita is once mentioned in the *Rigveda* as an earth goddess who blesses the land with good crops. In Vedic period, she was one of the goddesses associated with fertility. The *Kausik-sutra* and the *Paraskara-sutra* mention her repeatedly as the wife of Parjanya, a god associated with rains, and Indra. A Vedic hymn recites:

> Auspicious Sita, come thou near;
> We venerate and worship thee
> That thou mayst bless and prosper us
> And bring us fruits abundantly.

Some versions of the *Ramayana* suggest that Sita was a reincarnation of Vedavati, an orphan lady, who had been ravished by Ravana. According to a legend, sage Kushadhwaja was a learned and pious scholar residing in a remote hermitage. His daughter Vedavati grew up in her father's hermitage to become an ardent devotee of Vishnu. She has been described as a beautiful lady, dressed in the hide of a black antelope, her hair matted, and the bloom of her youth enchanted many prospective bridegrooms. Early in life, she resolved to wed only Vishnu. Her father refrained from stifling her aspirations and rejected proposals from many powerful kings and celestial beings. Vedavati continued to meditate upon Vishnu. Ravana, the ruler of Lanka, once found Vedavati seated in meditation and her beauty captivated his mind. He proposed to her, but she rejected him. Ravana mocked her austerities and her devotion to Vishnu. Frustrated in his attempts, he molested Vedavati. Vedavati immolated herself on a pyre. She vowed to return in another age and be the cause of Ravana's destruction. She was reborn as Sita, the wife of Rama, an incarnation of Vishnu. This episode has been related by sage Agastya in some versions of the *Ramayana*.

According to one, yet obscure version, originating in Kerala, Ravana and his wife Mandodari grew estranged from each other since Mandodari was repelled and distraught at her husband's ravishment of the hapless Vedavati. She soon found herself pregnant and feared that the child within her would be the harbinger of her husband's doom, as per Vedavati's awful oath. Despite her judgement of her husband, Mandodari could not condemn him and also could not do away with a child, even if her suspicions were confirmed, since fate could not be defied. Therefore, she went to her father's home in mainland India to prevent Ravana or anybody else from finding that she was pregnant. As the birth of the child grew near, Mandodari searched for a suitable foster home for her child. She discovered that Janaka, the pious king of Mithila, a man of noble character and eminent lineage, was childless; the deeply sorrowful king was intent upon performing a *yajna* to seek the boon of a child. At this juncture, a female child was born to Mandodari. Soon afterwards, just before Janaka began ploughing a field to prepare for the intended rituals, Mandodari managed to spirit her baby into the field and into Janaka's path. King Janaka discovered the child and adopted her. This legend is also related by Jains, which holds that Ravana's sin was primarily because of his evil actions towards his daughter.

Sita has been fully described in the *Ramayana* as the daughter of King Janaka, the ruler of Mithila, who had mastered knowledge enshrined in the scriptures and lived according to the tenets provided therein. The king was engaged in ritually ploughing the land to help produce food to counter a famine at that time. While using a golden plough, a pitcher appeared that had been buried. From this pitcher, Sita appeared. The plough tip was called a *sita*. In this way, the girl was named Sita. Since she was discovered in a ploughed field, she is also regarded as a daughter of *Bhumidevi*, the Earth Goddess. She was found and adopted by Janaka, king of Mithila (modern-day Janakpur, Nepal) and his wife Sunayana. At that time, the demon Ravana had collected tax from the local sages who had placed their blood in this pitcher. Thus, when the plough later was uncovered and churned the pitcher, the life force from the sages produced Sita. Sita thus became the cause of Ravana's destruction.

Sita grew young. One day, hoping to please an elderly maid, Sita quietly went into the room that the maid cleaned every day. The room had a huge bow given to King Janaka by Lord Shiva. It was so heavy that dozens of hefty soldiers were needed to inch it from its place. The maid saw that the bow now had been shifted to another place. The place where it had been kept for a long time had grown dirty, but it was now as clean as the other parts of the room. She was at her wits' end to guess who could have moved the massive thing. The king and the queen found that it was Sita who had shifted the bow and felt convinced that it was a divine sport (*leela*) of the Supreme Lord. King Janaka now decided to identify a match for her who could be equally brave.

Accordingly, King Janaka arranged a *swayamwara* to select a suitable husband for Sita. After her first glimpse of Lord Rama, Sita could no longer see him in the dense shrubbery. She glanced around with suppressed anxiety until one of her maids pointed them out. Seeing the captivating form, Sita felt as if she had found a long lost treasure. She forgot to blink and lost all consciousness of her body. She wanted to lock that lovely form into her heart. Her maids were quite aware of the drama being enacted before them. They teased Sita saying, 'This is not the time to meditate. Why don't you take a good look at these princes, Rama and Lakshmana? They have cast the spell of their beauty on all of us.' Visibly embarrassed, Sita opened her eyes and found both brothers in front of her. She prayed for the success of Lord Rama, the incarnation of Lord Vishnu, and then prince of Ayodhya, in bending the bow. The suitors present there tried their luck one by one. Ultimately, Lord Rama took the bow and immediately bent it as per the condition of King Janaka. Thus Lord Rama won Sita's hand in marriage.

But due to political intrigue, Rama's father, Dasharatha, had to keep a promise he had made to his second wife, Kaikeyi, who wanted her own son to ascend the throne and not Lord Rama. Therefore, she had Rama to be exiled and made him to wander through the forests of Dandakaranya. Rama requested Sita to stay back and serve his mothers in his absence, as she was likely to face many difficulties in the forest. At this, Sita said that there is no greater suffering than the parting from one's loved one. For her, Ayodhya would be meaningless without her husband. Husband's nearness mattered most to her. The very body, the wealth, the palace, the city, kingdom—all would give her only pain due to this parting. Pleasures would turn into illness and ornaments into burden. All her joy was in the company of her husband. The forests shall be her home, the animals shall be her companions, the mountains her palace, and this would happen only due to the company of her husband whom she loved. Thus Sita willingly renounced the comforts of the palace and joined her husband in braving through the travails of exile, while living in Dandakaranya. During that time, Ravana, who had all along been making efforts to bring Sita in wedlock with him and had even participated in the *swayamvara* but had failed, abducted her. He intruded into the place where Rama, Sita, and Lakshmana had been staying in the forest. Ravana disguised himself as a *sadhu* (mendicant) while her husband was away to fetch a magnificent golden deer to please her. This deer was actually Ravana's demon uncle, Mareecha, in disguise. Jatayu, the vulture-king, who was a friend of Rama, tried to protect her, but Ravana chopped off his wings. Jatayu survived long enough to inform Rama of what had happened. On the other hand, Ravana proposed Sita for marriage but she rejected the proposal. She also rejected his proposal to stay in his palace in Lanka (now, Sri Lanka). Thereupon, he kept Sita in the Ashoka Vatika, the garden of Ashoka trees and preserved her chastity.

Meanwhile, Rama and Lakshmana wandered the forests in search of Sita. They found out that she had been taken by Ravana and having learned where he was, Lord Rama deputed Hanuman, the monkey-god, to know the whereabouts of Sita. Hanuman, assuming the size of a mosquito, entered through one of the gates of Ashoka Vatika and carefully listened to the conversation between Ravana and Sita when she drew his attention to Lord Rama's power of arrows and called Ravana coward. When Ravana left, Sita begged the Ashoka tree to help her to find fire. Then she addressed the stars of the heaven to come down and burn her. On hearing this, tears welled up in Hanuman's eyes.

Hanuman met Sita and related to her all about Rama and his companion. He assured Sita that Rama's power would ultimately vanquish Ravana and his evil design. Finally, Lord Rama killed Ravana and his two brothers, thus rescuing Sita. After fourteen years of exile, Rama, Sita, Lakshmana, and Hanuman returned to Ayodhya where Rama was crowned King of Ayodhya. His father, Dasharatha, had already expired in his absence, and his brother Bharata had turned down his mother's offer to take over the throne of Ayodhya. He even met Rama in the forest to persuade him to return to Ayodhya to be the king. On his return to Ayodhya, after completing fourteen years of exile, Rama was crowned King with Sita by his side.

Lord Rama and Sita sat on a divinely resplendent throne, specially brought from Brahma for the occasion. While Rama's trust and affection for Sita never wavered, it soon became evident that a small section of Ayodhya could not accept Sita's long captivity under the power of Ravana.

According to a story, an intemperate washerman, while beating his wayward wife, declared that he was 'not Rama who would take his wife back after she had lived in the house of another man'. This statement was reported back to Rama, who knew that the aspersion cast on Sita was entirely baseless. Nevertheless, he felt his position as ruler undermined by the ever-present possibility of slander attaching itself to his hitherto unimpeachable dynasty and personal reign. It was this train of thought that led Rama to remove Sita from his household. Sita was again sent to exile. She was pregnant at this stage. She sought refuge in the hermitage of the sage Valmiki where she delivered twin sons, Luv and Kusha.

The two sons of Sita were brought up in the hermitage where Valmiki took care of their education. The boys grew up to be valiant and intelligent. They were eventually united with their father. Once she had witnessed the acceptance of her children by Rama, Sita sought final refuge in the arms of her mother *Bhumidevi*, the Earth Goddess. Hearing her plea for release from an unjust world and from a life that had rarely been happy, the earth dramatically split open. *Bhumidevi* manifested herself and took Sita away to a better world. But this part of the *Ramayana* is disputed. It is said that Rama and Sita lived together happily, ruling their kingdom for eleven thousand years, which had been a common lifespan at that time, the *Treta Yuga*. According to this version, Sita was only sent into a fourteen-year exile, one year of which she spent in Ravana's kingdom. In this way, it is generally considered that Rama and Sita had a perfectly happy married life and with very little disturbance. Some sages have disputed *Luv–Kush kanda*, and say that this was promoted by the British. Many Hindu organisations disown this part and state that crowning of Rama as king paved the way for *Ram Rajya* when everyone was happy.

It is believed that Sita also took part in the Hindu ritual of *Ashvamedha*, as narrated in the *Uttara Kanda*, Book 7, of the *Ramayana*. According to another version, Rama was married to a single wife, Sita, who, at that time, was not with him, having been excluded from Rama's capital of Ayodhya. She was, therefore, represented by a statue for the queen's ceremony. Sita was living in Valmiki's hermitage with her twin children, Luv and Kusha, whose birth was unknown to Rama. In its wanderings, the horse, accompanied by an army and the monkey king Hanuman, entered the forest and encountered Luv, who ignored the warning written on the horse's headplate. He tethered the horse, and Kusha challenged the army, which was unable to defeat the two brothers. It is also believed that this part of the story is written by the sage Valmiki in whose hermitage Sita took shelter.

In the *Ramayana*, Sita has been shown as an ideal Hindu wife. The vision and the voice of Valmiki are seen at their best while portraying the character of Sita as an ideal woman model for modesty, a symbol of sophisticated simplicity, an embodiment of grace and grandeur, a strict observer of ethical code of conduct, an exceptional example of supreme love, and a rare combination of course and compassion. She had a greater power of endurance than any other character in the *Ramayana*, except Rama. Rama and Sita were equal in this respect because every sorrow that affected the one affected the other as well, although they were situated in different environments. Hers was not the endurance of the stone or the wall, with no outside expression for the inner workings. These qualities make her a perfect match for the celebrated personality of Rama.

Again, in all her talks with Ravana, either before her capture or during her captivity in Lanka, Sita never hesitated to warn him fully of his danger. Her arguments were few, but she put them clearly and fearlessly before him. Even to Rama, as occasions arose, she talked with firmness and with dignity. Her first serious trial came when Rama advised her to stay in the palace with 'undisturbed mind', engaged in religious rites and fasts, and serving Dasharatha and Kausalya. Her patience was, in a way, rewarded, as Ravana was killed. But then came a bolt from the blue. The second instalment of forest life differed materially from the first. She was also at a loss to know how to answer the sages, if they asked her for what sin Rama had banished her. She could not think of jumping into the river as by committing suicide she would be terminating her husband's line of succession. Even in such a painful plight, the message she sent back through Lakshmana was clear and dignified. She wanted him to tell Rama that she considered it her duty to put a stop to any bad name that might come to him.

Years later, from the chanting of Luv and Kusha, Rama found out that Sita was alive. Although personally, he knew her to be chaste, and Valmiki publicly certified to the fact of her being pure, still Rama insisted on a second ordeal to convince all possible doubters. This time, there was no wider purpose to be served by Sita's continuing to remain with Rama, as Kusha and Luv had been accepted by Rama as his heirs. The line of succession was not in danger of extinction. Therefore, this time, when Sita invoked her purity, she asked only for a place within the earth. In all the important ceremonies, which Rama performed in later years, he kept by his side a golden image of Sita, as a visible representation of the ideal that accepted his heart all along.

Index

*9 7 8 8 1 2 9 1 1 8 2 5 7 *